Differentiated Parent Support

⚘

Engaging Parents in Unique Ways to
Increase Their Involvement in School

FRAN HJALMARSON

TurnAround Schools, Inc.

Differentiated Parent Support

Engaging Parents in Unique Ways to Increase Their Involvement in School

FRAN HJALMARSON

TurnAround Schools, Inc.

Special thanks to those who generously granted their permission to include their material in this book. All reasonable attempts have been made to obtain permission for the use of material quoted in the book. We regret any errors and omissions. If the owner of any material published in this book believes that such permission has not been granted, please contact us at TurnAroundSchools.com.

Information provided in this book is for informational purposes only and is not intended as professional advice. The author and publisher disclaim any responsibility for any liability, loss or risk incurred as a result, directly or indirectly, from the use of this book.

Names and identifying characteristics of individuals in this book have been changed.

This book was designed as a practical tool to assist educators in successfully creating a differentiated approach to working with the parents of each student. The forms and templates included in this book (and accompanying CD) were designed to assist educators toward this goal and as such can be downloaded and used as suggested in this book. Please keep in mind that these forms and templates, and any derivatives there of, are the copyrighted property of Fran Hjalmarson and TurnAround Schools. Thank you respecting our work.

ISBN: 978-0-9842154-1-6

Library of Congress Control Number: 2011929360

Available through
www.TurnAroundSchools.com

Printed in China

DEDICATION

To Grandma Meyer

My Child Whisperer

To My Husband

My Dream Carrier

To My Children

My Life Miracles

TABLE OF CONTENTS

Appendix
163

Bibliography
189

FOREWORD

In an age where test scores are king, the focus on the social and emotional needs of children and their families is often lost in the shuffle. Knowing this, many educators respond with knee-jerk reactions and shift priorities, making wellness the focal point of their school's mission. This too creates a challenge that, while it may be beneficial for the short-term emotional health of a student, is sure to widen the academic gap in years to come. If balance is the answer that schools must seek, what are the steps that need to be taken? How can today's schools pull off what others have failed to do for decades: to provide a positive social environment for children while at the same time delivering exceptional academic results? It is my belief that the answer to that question can be found right here in this book.

Fran Hjalmarson shares strategies that she has acquired over years as a counselor that are grounded not in theory, but in practice. Her experiences show that she knows how to support the social and emotional needs of children in a way that builds them up both as good people of character and as students committed to academic success. Just as Fran has helped to create a model for a positive school climate that others across the country are learning from, she is now tackling the vocal and silent perceptions that educators have about parents.

To help build a student up as an individual is a **commitment**. To work as diligently to ensure success for that student's family is a **gift**. Fran has a gift, and she shares it with us through these strategies and ideas that you can use daily to differentiate your support for parents. From the most pleasant moms and dads who step foot on campus, to the most challenging adults who storm into your office, these strategies will teach you how to find success by treating parents as individuals. Unique in her approach, Fran Hjalmarson will make you question the way you do business. Once you discover, like I did, that there are far better ways to connect with your families, you'll never wish for the past. If embraced, these strategies and ideas have the potential to revolutionize your school's climate and change the lives of your most needy students at the same time.

Damen Lopez
Founder
No Excuses University Network of Schools

ABOUT THIS BOOK

From the moment I became a counselor and stepped foot on the campus of my first school, my definition of parent involvement changed. As a parent myself, I assumed all parents were establishing routines, limiting TV, supporting homework, having conversations about school, and discussing goals and future careers after college. My idea of parent involvement was volunteering at school and working in the classroom.

Once I began working with students and families as an educator, I began to realize there are as many different parents as there are children. At one end of the spectrum are very capable and supportive parents while at the other end there are some that are completely "checked out." Recognizing that involved, supportive parents help to increase student success at school, one of the first priorities I began to focus on was understanding, defining, and positively impacting parent involvement.

This book is about my journey, ideas, and the strategies I developed to increase parent involvement in their child's education. I hope you will enjoy reading, but more importantly that you will discover new and effective methods to work with diverse parents to support student success.

Education is all a matter of building bridges.

~ Ralph Ellison

Key Concepts

1

Early Beginnings

2

Destiny can dramatically
alter the course of life

1

Destiny

"We plan our lives according to a dream that came to us in our childhood, and we find that life alters our plans. And yet, at the end, from a rare height, we also see that our dream was our fate. It's just that providence had other ideas as to how we would get there. Destiny plans a different route, or turns the dream around, as if it were a riddle, and fulfills the dream in ways we couldn't have expected."

~ Ben Okri

Destiny knows no permanence. It cares not about rarities, impossibilities, personal opinions, or desires. It is destiny, and it happens, once in a while or once in ten thousand. Which just so happened to be the odds that one little girl was up against.

More than fifty years ago, this little girl had a one in ten thousand chance at existence. After three births in three years, her overwhelmed mother had a tubal ligation, cutting and tying the fallopian tubes and removing the possibility of having any more children. Every once in a while, however, tubes come untied, grow back together, and a pregnancy occurs. This little girl was born unplanned to an already struggling family. Four years behind the three older siblings, this unwanted child was now the baby of the family. You can imagine how she was received by the already very chaotic household. Her mother did her best to provide equal time and attention to all four children, but the stress of the home always got in the way.

From the beginning, her older sister delighted in teasing her, telling her what many older siblings do, that she was found under a rock. Because she was the only blue-eyed member of the family, she actually thought that it might be true. Her sister would tease her until she cried and then take it a step further and laugh at her tears. The lack of attention and the constant tormenting by her older sister contributed to this now three-year-old little girl venturing off on her own and wandering through the neighborhood.

Pedals spinning, she powered a red tricycle as quickly as her little legs could pump. Escaping her chaotic home, she often lost herself in song. One day while singing and pedaling, she rounded the corner a block away from home. Suddenly she slowed as she caught a vision of an old woman watering her lawn. Approaching slowly, she studied the wrinkled face and saw the old woman's eyes crinkle into a smile. After a moment of studying each other, reluctantly, in a hushed tone, the little girl shyly smiled and said "Hello!" Her risk turned into reward as the seventy-five-year-old retired schoolteacher, with an even bigger smile, responded with a gentle "Well, hello there."

Gathering courage, the girl said, "You sure have a pretty blue dress." The old woman cordially replied, "Thank you." When the little girl noticed her snow-colored hair, she made a comment about how pretty and white it was. The woman smiled and chuckled as if she were amused.

As the little one continued to gaze at the old woman, she took note of her glasses. They were rimless and looked just like glasses that a grandmother might wear. She began to think of the one grandmother she never knew and the other whom she rarely saw. Longing for connections and attention, she wished that this woman could be her grandma. As she continued to daydream, a thought came to mind and she blurted out, "Can I call you grandma?" Flattered by the question, the woman offered a smile and a nod of her head. In this instant, a life-altering relationship began between the old woman, Grandma Meyer, and the little girl, myself. I had found a safe sanctuary.

The initial visits between Grandma Meyer and me began on the red steps of her front porch. Daily we would meet on the steps and visit. We would talk about books, family, and life. As our relationship blossomed, the steps led onto the front porch, where we would sit for hours visiting, reading, and drawing. Our bond continued to grow, and eventually I began spending time inside the house. Sometimes we would bake in the kitchen and other times we would work on puzzles together. Every visit involved opening my world through experiences and characters found in books. In fact, "Grandma Meyer" was able to teach me to read even before I entered kindergarten. When I started school as a five-year-old, my mother began to work at the county courthouse and asked Grandma Meyer to take care of me every day after school.

She was happy to have a little girl in her life and willingly agreed to pick me up every day at school and keep me safely in her home. About halfway through the year, I began to spend the night. It wasn't long before I started to live with Grandma Meyer full-time, just around the corner from my biological family. My parents would pick me up every Friday evening on the way home from work and then drop me off every Sunday afternoon to my "new home." I had my own bedroom, wardrobe, toys, and books. I had found a safe sanctuary to be cared for and loved. This became my "new normal," to live with a neighbor whom I now called "Grandma," and to visit my biological family on the weekends. It wasn't until one of my uncles inquired about it one weekend when I was seven years old that I began to question this unusual arrangement. Why didn't my mom and dad want me? Did they like the other three kids better? Had I done something wrong? Did they miss me when I wasn't there? These questions went unasked and unanswered.

On holidays, I would begin my day with my biological family and then spend the rest of my afternoon and evening with my adopted family. When the Meyers would travel to their farm in Iowa every other summer for a month, I happily joined them. I had become so comfortable with the Meyer family that I often preferred to be with them. When they spent weekends in Carmel, California, I was the first one in the car. When I was old enough for dance lessons, Grandma Meyer took me to the studio. When it was necessary to go to the dentist, Grandma Meyer took me there as well. I was loved and cared for as if I was one of her own. This nurturing was consistent until I was twelve years old.

In 1971, Grandpa Meyer, who lived in Iowa to care for the family farm, fell ill. Grandma Meyer was forced to move. With no options, I moved back in with my biological family. It was a very difficult transition and couldn't have come at a worse time with the onset of adolescence! Because my mom and dad were working full-time, I was often unsupervised. There were times, however, when I was left in the care of my nineteen-year-old sister. Unfortunately, she was on a very dangerous path that included the use of drugs and other high-risk behaviors. As often happens with teens on dangerous paths, they like to take people with them. Thus, as a very young adolescent of twelve, I was introduced to drugs. With the encouragement of my older sister, I began to experiment with many different drugs that were supplied by her. In an instant, life for me became very dark. Without the stability of Grandma Meyer, and lacking the supervision of my parents, my life began spiraling out of control. I participated in some of the most inappropriate and even dangerous encounters of my life. Desperately searching for love and stability, I fell victim to a nineteen-year-old male predator who took advantage of my vulnerability and robbed me of my innocence. Not long after, I felt very hopeless and lost and longed for change.

Just when following in my sister's footsteps was becoming my reality, my path took a turn for the better as my life intersected with a church youth group. With the guidance, support, and strong intervention of group leaders, I was able to get off this self-destructive path and reshape my life. I successfully finished high school and went to college. That is the beginning of my story and my first incident with a significant experience that totally changed the path of my life and ultimately my destiny.

The decision to become an educator was in a large part due to my early experiences and challenges. Knowing what it is like to be a child dealing with adversity and experiencing challenges that affected my readiness to learn, I developed a strong desire to be able to work with children in similar situations, particularly those children whose path may never cross with someone like Grandma Meyer. I now know that these children have tremendous potential for success if they are provided the same support and guidance that I was able to receive. Thus my decision to become a school counselor was a natural fit.

The act of working with parents and their children is not just a job for me. It's who I am and what I have become grounded in. It's my passion and my life's work. It is my destiny.

Theory to Practice

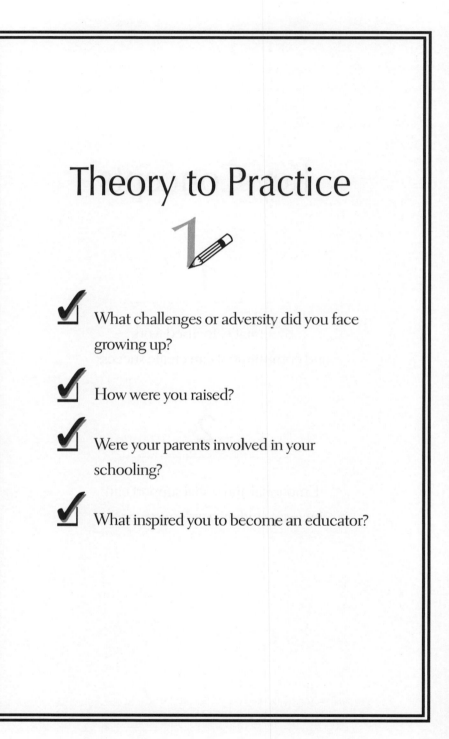

✓ What challenges or adversity did you face growing up?

✓ How were you raised?

✓ Were your parents involved in your schooling?

✓ What inspired you to become an educator?

Key Concepts

1

Systematic, focused work
and commitment can create success

2

Emotional and social support can
increase student academic success

2

One School's Story

"Never doubt that a small group of thoughtful, committed citizens can change the world. Indeed it's the only thing that ever has."

~ Margaret Mead

In 2003, I was perfectly happy splitting my time as a counselor at two elementary schools when my boss informed me that I was being reassigned. Not only did I not want to have to make a change and leave the school communities I was working with, I was being transferred to a school whose reputation preceded it as one of the most challenging in the district. In fact, many of my colleagues at the time sarcastically wished me luck, saying, "Those parents are going to be tough to work with!"

Los Peñasquitos, fondly referred to as Los Pen, is one of six Title

I schools within the mostly affluent Poway Unified School District in San Diego, California. PUSD serves 30,000 students in twenty-three elementary schools, five middle schools, and five comprehensive high schools. Los Pen, however, has always drawn from a steady base of low-income families. To the south of the school is a neighborhood of middle-income single-family homes, while to the north are two sizeable apartment complexes. These apartments combine for the largest federally funded Section-8 housing complex in North San Diego County. Such demographics drove pessimistic perceptions of the school that in turn fostered negative results. For years, decades in fact, Los Pen was frowned upon by others as it was consistently the lowest performing school in our district. How bad were the results?

In California, schools are measured by something called an Academic Performance Index, or API Score. A score above 800 is good, but an API more than 900 is exceptional. Below 800 is considered unacceptable, leaving schools that remain in the 700s in jeopardy of moving into program improvement as part of "No Child Left Behind." In 1997, Los Pen was at a dismal 726. Not only was the school the lowest performing school in the Poway district, but every subgroup was performing very poorly. In short, the students were not learning to their potential. Unfortunately, this underachievement was not always challenged or questioned. After all, the school had a population that represented thirty-eight different languages and where 43 percent of the children came from poverty. In addition, this highly transient population also included hundreds of second language learners who made up more than a third of the school's enrollment. With demographics like these, many asked, "How could a staff be expected to have any type of success with these children?"

While the staff loved, cared, and worked very hard to teach students, there was an unspoken yet accepted belief that this was simply the best that they could do. It became the status quo. Many of the students had very little support outside of the regular school day. Additionally, many of the parents were not involved in their children's education whatsoever, which offered a convenient excuse that added to the acceptance of poor performance for decades. There were at times flashes of success, but on the whole, the challenges of the school were abundant and pervasive. What was unknown to me and many others, however, was the positive trend that was slowly and quietly taking shape during the years that led up to my move to the school.

In 1997, Jeff King was appointed as the new principal of Los Peñasquitos Elementary School. Working closely together, Jeff and the staff began to eradicate the mistaken belief that those children couldn't learn and began to go about creating what is now referred to as a culture of universal achievement. This culture of universal achievement is based on the beliefs that **all** children can learn and that it is the **staff's** job to teach them. Jeff's influence made a powerful and long-lasting impact that began to move Los Pen in a positive direction. His leadership was followed up five years later by a new principal named Damen Lopez.

While Jeff helped shape the belief that impacted the school's culture, Damen didn't just embrace the belief but also began to work with the staff to build *exceptional systems* focusing on collaboration, standards alignment, assessment, data analysis, and interventions (King and Lopez, 2008). The combined focus, passion, and commitment on the part of the "new and improved" approach was absolutely amazing. Rather than having fifteen different goals, Los Pen pursued excellence with one overarching goal, that "All students will become proficient in reading, writing, and math." This radical shift led to tremendous academic gains. By the early 2000s, Los Pen's API moved out of the 700s and into the 800s. Every year, the test scores and, more importantly, individual proficiency levels continued to progress. In 2008, Los Pen earned a whopping 917 on the state's Academic Performance Index. While this is nothing less than amazing, what is even more incredible is the comparison between Los Pen's results and similar schools in California. When compared to the 100 schools most similar in the state, Los Pen has been in the top 10 percent eight out of the last ten years, and number one on list the last four consecutive years!

While Los Pen has gone from being the lowest performing school in the district academically to one of the highest in the state of California, the neighborhood has not changed. Nor have the social challenges. The students deal with the same issues they always have. The parents continue to struggle with the grip of poverty, and the neighborhood's demographics continue to present great obstacles for student success. And while the shifts in academic culture did lead to terrific results beginning in 1997, the fact is that the possibilities for positive change related to the social culture were left untapped. Which, as it so happens, was exactly why my boss transferred me there in 2003.

Social Support as a Means of Academic Gains — Really?

I'll never forget the first time I met Damen Lopez. We were

attending a kick-off meeting before the school year began. The room was filled with principals, counselors, district leaders, school psychologists, and other district directors. My boss, Elaine, suggested I find Damen and introduce myself to him as the new counselor of Los Pen. Let me tell you, I was less than thrilled but knew that I had to resign myself to the change and try to make the best of it. As I looked over toward him, I am sure that he could read from my expression that I was not very enthusiastic. I was surprised to see that he wasn't looking so enthusiastic, either. As it turns out, he liked the counselor who was leaving and wasn't any happier about the change than I was. We shook hands and that was it. Little did we know that it was the beginning of a very fruitful path — the path of success for a struggling school.

This incredible success at Los Pen happened with the hard work and dedication of an amazing staff that had a strict focus on academics. They worked together, creating a culture of universal achievement and exceptional systems. Damen's lone directive to me was this: Whatever you do to support the social and emotional needs of our students must never get in the way of their academic success. I eased Damen's mind by not only agreeing with him but guaranteeing him that I could help improve the academic success of the school by developing exceptional systems around social and emotional support. The look in his eyes when I offered the guarantee said, "Woman, you must be out of your mind!" Nonetheless, he trusted me, and I immediately began working with the students, parents, and staff right away.

At the time, the school already had almost every staff member working very hard on several exceptional systems focused on academics, so I decided to start with a team of three. The School Climate Committee met every week to discuss a variety of topics spotlighting the social and emotional needs of students and their families. We chose to concentrate specifically on student behavior and parent involvement. As we brainstormed and came up with ideas, we would then present those ideas to the staff for feedback and input before implementing. Because systems only work if people use them, the collaboration with staff was vital for a successful outcome. Over the course of the year, the committee worked with the staff to create a classroom and school-wide management system based on character. I helped to teach the staff that consequences don't change behavior; explicit teaching does. The success was seen by all, and the buy-in for the work of the School Climate Committee was evident.

Today, the School Climate Committee has evolved into a larger group with a representative from each grade level, the principal, and the counselor. Because many of the strategies to enhance parent involvement and improve student behavior are now implemented with the support of all staff, the committee now primarily serves the purpose of monitoring and evaluating effectiveness. It's a great place to be! Blending effective academic exceptional systems with social and emotional systems that support students and families is one of the most underestimated tools a school can use to increase the overall success of a campus. But don't take my word for it. Just look at the trends that began in 2003 and continue to this day.

In the first year that we implemented our initial social and emotional systems, we reduced the discipline referrals to the office by 43 percent.

When students are sent to the office, they miss out on being in the classroom and learning. Most incidents remove a student from the classroom for a minimum of half an hour. By decreasing the discipline referrals, we increased academic time. As the systems took hold in the first year, there was a thirty-five-point jump in API. Student success has continued to increase every year.

The success that began with a group of caring educators on one campus has become a source for change at schools across the country. As shared in the book *No Excuses University* by Damen Lopez, Los Peñasquitos Elementary's story has inspired a movement that blends academic and social success for kids under the umbrella of college readiness. The No Excuses University Network of Schools was created for like-minded professionals who want to exchange ideas that ultimately help to foster hope for some of our country's neediest children. What began at Los Pen has now become a network of 92 schools that represents more than 50,000 students in 15 different states. I believe Damen says it best: "This effort must be one that finds every opportunity to support every stakeholder in the community. To lack the diligence of offering support to our parents, or to make excuses for our own failures to succeed based on a lack of involvement by them, is to count our students out before they even open up a book, are taught a lesson from their teacher, or learn to interact with their peers."

The Los Peñasquitos and No Excuses University story is a powerful one that is focused solely on the academic success of students. And while this success is the ultimate goal, some are often naïve about just how much the partnership with our parents has contributed to today's outcomes. In addition, others are misinformed about what it takes to create such a partnership. This is why I have written this book. The first step is to avoid what I believe to be the biggest trap that exists in public education: the parent trap.

Theory to Practice

 Think about your school staff. Are there attitudes or perceptions toward parents that are inhibiting your ability to support an increase in parent involvement? What are your traps?

 What kinds of things has your staff purposefully done to increase parent involvement?

 What are you willing to do to support parent involvement?

Key Concepts

1

Negative attitudes and perceptions hinder
a school's ability to work effectively with parents

2

We need to get out of the "Parent Trap" and change
our approach with parents

3

The Parent Trap

"When elephant steps on a trap, no more trap."

~ African Proverb

As educators, we are often caught in what I refer to as the parent trap. This is the belief that educators fall into by thinking that everything is the parents' fault. We make assumptions that parents, even those in poverty, are equally capable of teaching children in the same manner that a trained educator is. This happens to even our best educators. They are trapped by "stinking thinking" when it comes to parents and their involvement in their children's education. For years we have been taught, almost subliminally, that parents are the problem. Have you ever been caught in the parent trap? Take this short test.

Caught in the Parent Trap?

Ask yourself if you have ever said or accepted any of the following statements:

- If the parents would only read to them at home, the students would do much better.

- If the students would just get enough sleep at home, they would perform better.

- If they were fed properly, it would make a huge difference.

- If Mom or Dad would help on homework, the students would learn more.

- If they spoke English at home, it would make my job so much easier.

- If they taught them right from wrong, these kids wouldn't be so hard to teach.

- If the parents would just take some parenting classes, they would be better parents.

- If the parents reduced television/video game time, the kids would be more interested in reading.

- If the parents would just monitor what children are watching on TV, the students would behave better.

So how did you do on the quiz? If you are like me, even you are guilty of thinking, saying, or simply accepting such beliefs from colleagues over the years. Such sayings begin as venting but often turn into a deeply grounded belief among educators. It becomes a trap when we listen to these sayings and do nothing. If we do nothing and listen in silence, we condone what people are saying and also send the message that we agree with what they are saying. This gives them the courage to continue the negativity and permeates the campus with poisonous beliefs about parents.

In the end, the parent trap consistently whispers in our ear, "You're not the problem; it's the parents. You can only do so much, so don't be so hard on yourself." In time, educators release themselves from responsibility and place all of the blame on parents for their lack of involvement. What happens after that? The kids lose every time.

Stomping Out the Parent Trap

To successfully work with parents, we need to free ourselves from the trap of thinking negatively about parents and using it as an excuse to do nothing. Tough situations and long-standing practices often take a very large action, as large as an elephant, to make a change. With this in mind, here are four ways in which we can remove the parent trap for good.

Recognize the Trap: In our lives, we have good habits and we have bad habits. What keeps such habits going? We are either given praise and approval for the positive things that we do, or confronted by the negative routines that we exhibit. The same holds true for our practices as professionals. Most of the time, our excuse-making when it comes to parents is simply a result of habit, a habit we fail to recognize because we are often surrounded by others who are caught in the same pattern of behavior. The first step in getting out of the parent trap is to recognize what it is and ask yourself whether it is helping or harming students.

Manage Expectations: In fairness to those in our profession, when it comes to our most at-risk students, have we ever been taught any differently when it comes to parents being the problems? Think of all the training that you went through to become a teacher. How many courses did you take that focused on reaching the hard-to-reach student in spite of what took place at home? If you are like me, the answer is none. Teaching programs focus on the classroom and students. Yet we know that parents can be a big piece of the puzzle when it comes to student learning. Study after study validates that students can be more successful when parents are involved. Yet teachers at many schools, particularly Title I schools, struggle with the lack of parent involvement and throw their hands up in defeat. They take an all or nothing approach. While it would be a dream come true, school staffs must understand that dynamic academic gains for students will likely never take place solely by what happens in an at-risk home. No amount of help on homework from a parent who might be illiterate is going to improve a student's grades in school. No well-balanced breakfast is going to cure every issue that a student has with attention in class. The real gains for students, especially those who are at-risk, will be a result of strategies that are deployed on campus coupled with a limited set of expectations for how parents can help at home.

Change Our Approach with Parents: A big part of the problem is in the way that we continue to work with and treat parents. Educators often treat all parents exactly alike, when in reality, parents are as varied and as diverse as our students. Just as with teaching diverse students, we need to be more systematic in our approach to parent support and involvement.

Set a Goal, Make a Plan: When school staffs set a goal to positively impact parent involvement yet fail to create a plan to meet the needs of these diverse parents, they are setting themselves up for failure. Don't just set a goal without an action plan. That's just a dream or a wish. If we taught students that way, we would be miserable failures. If we sat around and wished our students would learn to read or learn their math facts but never used assessments and made plans, we would most certainly fail. When it comes to parent involvement, just as with teaching, we need to set a goal and then create a plan and system to reach that goal. Is it easy? Of course not! It's a lot of hard work, but it is critical. The most effective path to success is a systematic approach. It can be done in five steps:

1. Define parent involvement.

2. Understand parents' challenges and barriers to parent involvement.

3. Create solutions that will eliminate, reduce, or neutralize the barriers.

4. Implement solutions and programs to support parent involvement.

5. Evaluate and monitor success.

Confronting the parent trap is not easy. In fact, it requires us to rebuild our belief system brick by brick about parents, their role in their children's education, and how we work closely to partner with them on a daily basis. Recognizing the trap that we are caught in gives us a base to rebuild upon. Managing expectations and being willing to change our approach offers us two handy tools to get the job done. Finally, making a plan, or systematic approach, as a means to achieving a goal will give us the direction that we need to get the job done. In the chapters ahead you will be given practical strategies to rebuild your approach with parents, as individuals, in a way that will increase student success and change the perceptions that exist about how parents should be involved and supported on your campus.

Theory to Practice

 Evaluate whether you and your colleagues are in the parent trap.

 What can you do to change the way you think about parents?

 Set a goal for parent involvement.

Key Concepts

1

Parent involvement needs to be defined

2

Three areas of parent involvement

3

Parent involvement enhances student success

4

What is Parent Involvement?

"Children are not casual guests in our home. They have been loaned to us temporarily for the purpose of loving them and instilling a foundation of values on which their future lives will be built."

~ Dr. James Dobson

When you think of parent involvement, what comes to your mind? Do you picture a mom who actively supports the PTA? Maybe you think of a dad who volunteers in the classroom from time to time. Or maybe, for some, it's just about parents helping raise money for a school. As a parent, when my girls entered kindergarten, my belief was a mixture of all three. Even after my kids were grown and into my first years as a school counselor, my concept of parent involvement remained the same. Simply put, parent involvement was about PTA and volunteering.

Early in my career, I was working at an affluent school where we didn't have to worry about trying to engage parents. In fact, in some cases we were more concerned about parent over-involvement. You know the ones I'm talking about. These are the parents who do too much for their children and keep them from developing a sense of independence. They're the ones who jump in too soon, rescuing them from failure while at the same time stifling opportunities that might lead to children learning through their mistakes. From poverty to affluence, every school has parents like these.

After being transferred to Los Peñasquitos Elementary School, my concept of parent involvement radically changed. As I began working with Title I students and their families, I realized there were numerous layers of parent involvement that went well beyond PTA and volunteering. In fact, I found several other areas of parent involvement that were far more significant in translating to overall student success. In time, I shaped a definition that included three essential aspects of parent involvement: parental support, parental engagement, and parental participation. We believe that every parent, regardless of their socioeconomic or cultural background, can fit into one of these categories. So much so that at Los Pen and many No Excuses University schools across the country, we introduce these concepts to all parents at an annual meeting we refer to as the NEU Parent Forum (the details of which can be found in Chapter Five). This forum sets the stage for our expectations of parents as we teach them, in an explicit way, how they can partner with the school in a meaningful way.

PARENTAL SUPPORT

Parental support is student-driven. Parents get involved as a result of students' actions and initiative. Parents encourage their children's positive behavior and find ways to enhance their overall academic and school success. Many parents automatically provide this support, but some may still need to be taught. Because what takes place at home is at the core of parental support, it's about teaching parents how to get involved on a daily basis.

Meaningful Dialogue

The first thing that we teach parents is as simple as having a conversation. All of us need to talk to our children every day about school. Holding conversations with students about routines, expectations, and particularly about what they learned is a fundamental necessity to encourage improvement. We can engage in conversations about what their day was like, what they found challenging in class, what skills they believe they have mastered and struggle with, or the academic goals that they have set with their teacher. Parents must discuss friendships and social interactions in nurturing ways that open the door to provide guidance to children. These conversations need to be what I like to refer to as meaningful dialogue.

Meaningful dialogue is when we experience thoughtful interactions during a conversation. It is not about barking directions such as "get your homework done," "wash up for dinner," or "help clear the table." It is not about "grilling" someone for answers. Meaningful dialogue happens when we engage in asking and responding to what, why, and how questions, posed in a way that causes reflection on the part of children. These are not passive questions that can be answered with a simple "yes" or "no." Because of this, we don't want to ask children, "Did you have a good day?" Instead we ask, "What was the best or hardest part of your day?" Meaningful dialogue must also follow up with questions such as "What could you do about that next time it happens?" "What would have happened if you had made a different choice?" or "What were you feeling when that happened?" These are questions that engage children in thinking and encourage them to respond with answers that support self-evaluation. These conversations are incredibly valuable because they build a learning relationship between parent and child. Because many parents from all different backgrounds are untrained in having these types of conversations, it must be explicitly taught. To support parents in this daily conversation, Los Pen came up with a concept that we call Take Five. While you will read more about Take Five in Chapter Six, in short it is a five-minute, five-step conversation that we teach every parent to have with their children on a daily basis. At Los Pen, we introduce Take Five to parents at the NEU Forum. Other NEU schools offer similar meaningful dialogue templates to their parents as well.

Setting Reasonable Expectations

Another aspect of parental support that we endorse is the act of setting reasonable expectations. Parents need to work with their children to create reasonable expectations for behavior and academic success. What do I mean by reasonable? The expectations need to be appropriate for the developmental age and ability of the individual child. These expectations must be openly discussed, encouraged, and reinforced. For example, most kindergarten students are capable of packing their backpacks, getting dressed, and working on homework independently. They are capable of understanding and following the rules at home and school. Thus parents need to have these conversations with their children and establish clear, reasonable expectations for them to follow through on.

Establishing Routines

Just like teachers, parents must establish crystal-clear routines. Setting up routines for getting up on time, preparing for school, arriving from home, and completing homework all enhance student success. Establishing routines that help kids prep for dinner or bedtime are crucial as they develop responsibility. Children do better with structure and routines because they create consistency and stability for them. They feel safe and secure when they know what is expected of them and also of others. The predictability of their routine and schedule helps them to learn responsibility, gain confidence, and ultimately contributes to their success. While it may be necessary to sometimes be flexible with routines, teaching parents to be faithful to them as much as possible fosters the greatest support for children. In the event that routines need to change, it is important that parents clearly communicate the change to children. Some areas where routines are crucial are:

Supporting Homework

It is essential that any afternoon routine include the completion of homework and a time for reading. Parents need to actively support homework by providing and enforcing homework time as part of their daily afternoon routine. Parents need to help students establish a quiet place to work and provide encouragement and support during homework time within close proximity of their homework location. They don't need to have their own personal desk. A corner of the kitchen table or counter, along with a shoebox of supplies, works just as well. The location just needs to be established and consistently utilized. Part of the homework plan must include reading daily, whether assigned by teachers or not. Reading daily is particularly important for elementary-age students, who are still working on their reading skills and developing their love of reading. While typically part of a bedtime routine, daily reading can just as easily take place at another time. The most important thing is to read, read, read. Reading is the entry to all other areas of an academic career.

Organizing Space

Another important piece of children's routines needs to include a single location for school necessities, such as backpacks, lunch pails, library books, jackets, and schoolwork. Maybe it's near the front door or perhaps it's the dining room table.

Limits on Media

All children's daily routines also must include limits on TV viewing and video games. We hear from pediatricians and psychologists all the time that children view far too much TV and spend too much time playing video games. The American Academy of Pediatrics website has loads of articles available about the effects of television viewing for children. Most experts agree that children should not be viewing any more than two hours of TV every day, yet statistics often reveal a much higher rate. According to the American Academy of Child and Adolescent Psychiatry, children in the United States watch an average of three to four hours of television a day. By high school graduation, they will have spent more time watching television than they have in the classroom! Television is very passive, and children miss out on opportunities to be more active intellectually, artistically, and physically. Time spent watching television takes away from important activities such as reading, school work, playing, exercise, family interaction, and social development. Watching television has also been associated with attention problems in children. A recent study, "Television and Video Game Exposure and the Development of Attention Problems," published in the August 2010 print issue of *Pediatrics*, found a similar effect for video games:

> *Researchers assessed 1,323 children in third, fourth and fifth grades over 13 months, using reports from the parents and children about their video game and television habits, as well as teacher reports of attention problems. Another group of 210 college students provided self-reports of television habits, video game exposure and attention problems. Researchers found children who exceeded the 2 hours per day of screen time recommended by the American Academy of Pediatrics were 1.5 to 2 times more likely to be above average in attention problems.*

Until more research is done about the effects of screen time on very young children, the American Academy of Pediatrics strongly discourages television viewing for children ages two years old or younger and encourages interactive play. For older children, the Academy advises no more than one to two hours per day of educational, nonviolent programs, which should be supervised by parents or other responsible adults in the home.

Attendance

One of the most important aspects of parental support is getting kids to school every day on time unless they are sick. Attendance is so critical to student success, and helping all parents understand this is our job. In our NEU Parent Forum, we talk about attendance and discuss the term soft truancy. Soft truancy pertains to all of the unnecessary absences. We need to ensure that parents comprehend how critical it is to have students at school, on time every day. In Chapter Six, I discuss a meeting that we refer to as a Parent Forum. Attendance is a big piece of the Parent Forum and an opportunity for us to articulate just how important attendance is to academic success. We share our school's attendance and academic data and compare it to the highest-performing elementary school in our district. The data shows that the highest performing school of our twenty-three schools is also the school with the very best attendance rates. No surprise there! We use this opportunity to teach parents how important attendance is to student success.

Teachable Moments

If we genuinely want to change parent involvement, then we need to maximize every teachable moment to help parents understand how to support their children in school. Just as with students, parents come in all shapes, sizes, and abilities. For those parents who don't innately have the skills, we create opportunities to explicitly teach them. Chapters Six, Seven, and Eight are filled with ideas and strategies to teach parents how to become more involved and engaged in their children's academic success.

PARENTAL ENGAGEMENT

At the core of parental engagement is a partnership that exists between home and school. Rather than the students driving the support, when it comes to engagement it is the parents' action that is primary. Parental support is about helping a child at home, but parental engagement is about parents becoming a part of the school community. As you will see, there are many opportunities for parents to get engaged.

The first thing that school staffs must do to foster such engagement is to create a welcoming environment so that parents feel encouraged to be a part of the school community. Have you ever walked into a place of business, been treated rudely, and then vowed to never step foot on the premises again? Thousands of parents across the country have had similar experiences walking through the front doors of their children's schools. And because many adults today harbor negative feelings toward school due to their own experiences as children, we cannot risk them feeling discouraged as parents. Unless parents feel comfortable and welcomed, they are not going to fully engage in their child's education. This is an area that is too often overlooked and where very little training is provided. Schools must make this a top priority and provide training on how their staffs can engage parents.

Establishing Relationships

The training of a staff must include the use of strategies to establish relationships with parents. All of us have different levels of social skills. For some people, connecting with others is easy and comes very naturally. For many, it's a tremendous challenge and avoided at all costs. As schools, we need to deliberately teach our staff members how to both develop relationships with parents and foster a welcoming environment for them. Below are a few examples of how this might look on your campus:

- ◆ Within the first few weeks of school, connect with every parent in person, on the phone, or by email.

- ◆ Send weekly or bi-weekly notes about what things are happening in the classroom.

- ◆ Share good news with phone calls, postcards, or emails.

- ◆ Greet parents in line or at the classroom door.

- ◆ Be available to parents. Parents may want to have an extended conversation at an inappropriate time (when teachers are trying to start the school day or when other people are present, for example). To avoid parents feeling brushed off, have a simple form available for parents to complete. Tell parents you want to speak with them when you can give all of your attention to the conversation and that you will contact them at the end of the school day to find a time that works for everyone.

◆ Listen to parents and check for understanding before responding.

◆ After a parent meeting is over, if there are several school staff members in attendance, leave the meeting room together. If staff members stay behind after parents leave, parents may feel that they are being talked about. If staff members need to recap the meeting, gather together in another location.

There are also actions that can be taken as a school. The school office needs to be a welcoming atmosphere for parents. When they walk into the office, parents need to be greeted as quickly as possible. Even when the office is busy, give them a quick acknowledgement that they have been noticed and a comment that someone will be right with them. Treating parents with courtesy and almost like they are a customer goes a long way in establishing relationships of mutual respect.

School activities also need to be welcoming to parents. Hold informal and friendly events. There are simple things schools can do that don't take much time or money. For example, Horace Mann Middle School in Amarillo, Texas purchased doughnuts one morning. As parents were dropping their children off at school, the sidewalk was lined with teachers who greeted each parent with a smile, a "hello," and a doughnut. Parents were surprised and pleased and, since that simple action, have initiated the smiles and "hello" at the curbside drop-off.

Consistent Communication

Another area of parental engagement is communication. Schools need to design effective forms of open communication between the home and school that relate to on-campus programs as well as student progress. This includes creating a regular schedule for useful notices (both academic and behavior), phone calls, newsletters, and other forms of communication that are sent home throughout the year. (Templates for such communication can be found in the appendix.) In addition, we need to constantly offer new and creative opportunities for teachers to communicate in positive ways. If the only time a parent ever hears from the teacher or school is when there is a problem, what encourages them to pick up the phone the next time the caller ID says the school name on it? I recognize that teachers and school staff have very full plates and are "time challenged," but we need to find ways to go the extra mile for those parents who are tough to engage. I've found that you can realize a great return on your investment by taking two minutes to send a quick postcard, voicemail, or note home. Even better still, send an email.

Communicating in the 21st Century

You would be amazed at how many schools today lack the basic strategies to use email, both on and off campus. I know it sounds crazy, but trust me, it exists every day at schools across the country. As you think about using the digital age to enhance your communication, you will always come up with naysayers who love to say, "But our poor families don't have access to these tools!" In my experience, this is the furthest thing from the truth. Don't believe me? Try this little experiment. Walk to the homes or apartments of some of your students living in poverty. I'd be willing to bet that the first thing you see is a big screen TV hooked up to cable, and a computer that not only has internet access, but high speed internet access. It has been my experience that, while having limited means, families living in poverty tend to spend a good portion of their money on entertainment. This is something that we need to capitalize on, and it begins with emails.

Now I could write paragraphs on this topic, but it would waste your time as a reader. When it comes to email, principals must make sure that every teacher gathers the email addresses of every parent at the beginning of the year. Teach teachers how to make a group email on their computers, and hold them accountable for consistently communicating with parents. Our rule: If a parent contacts you via email, you should respond within 24 hours. Of course, we must always remember that the tone of an email is found in the eyes of the reader, so if there's something serious that must be shared, do so in person. All in all, you will save time and become far more efficient.

In addition, having a school website is great, but unless it is up-to-date it isn't effective in the least. Online software tools can be linked to any site and can help enhance consistent communication with parents, allowing them to review student grades, check on attendance data, and access important classroom announcements. In an effort to both support parents who don't have their own computers as well as draw them on campus, some NEU schools are coming up with innovative options.

Take San Jacinto Elementary School in Amarillo, Texas. San Jacinto provides two computers in the front office for parents to use. In Reno, Nevada, the Washoe County School District is using grant funding to create kiosks throughout the community for parents to have access to their student information. When updating computers, some districts reimage computers and provide them to low-income families for free. If you are truly committed to enhancing communication with parents, think outside the box and get creative.

Modeling

Understanding and modeling the school rules at home reinforces the appropriate behavior for academic success. Similar expectations at school and home create consistency for children. Schools can share the rules at the Parent Forum meeting at the beginning of the year and include them in a parent handbook (seen in the appendix) that is given to all parents. As parents and staff members model behavior, it is critical for them to reinforce the importance of continued learning and the value of hard work. Parents can do this by continuing to expand their own knowledge, attending classes that a school can offer. Parent education classes and seminars are taking place daily on NEU campuses across the country, with terrific results. One class that is offered at many of our schools is "The Value of Setting Goals with Your Children." Parents are taught to not only encourage the act of goal setting, but model it by sharing their own personal goals with their children.

These conversations about goals can include the creation of future goals, which then becomes a positive habit that is established both in school and at home. Discussions about what they want to be when they grow up can then lead to conversations about college and the importance of earning a degree. Years ago, parents used to push for high school graduation. It became an expectation. They would

40

have conversations and say things such as "When you graduate from high school . . ." Because the world has changed so much, the expectations and dialogue also need to change. Now it needs to be, "When you graduate from college . . ." As Damen Lopez's book *No Excuses University* and current U.S. Census data suggests, in today's world people with a college education are more financially successful. Having parents begin the discussions about college in elementary school is a great way to plant the seeds of success.

PARENTAL PARTICIPATION

In the area of parent participation, the actions of the parents are primary. Parents who participate are actively engaged in a variety of ways. Parents attend school events, particularly the events focused on academic success or enhancing parenting skills. Attending other social events, such as movie nights, festivals, carnivals, and school potlucks, is also part of parent participation.

Volunteering is included in parent participation. Parents who are actively engaged find many ways to volunteer. They help out in the classroom, library, or other places on campus. For some parents, their time is limited by work or other commitments, and they are not able to participate in this way. Thus some parents who still want to volunteer do so by taking work home for teachers and returning it upon completion.

Parents in this category are the first to volunteer for a variety of committees organized by the school or district. From parent-teacher associations to human relations organizations to budget committees, these parents are actively involved as they help to make decisions that improve the education of students. These parents are also the most likely to participate in activities well outside the campus lines. These activities could include things like cleaning up the community, helping feed the homeless, packaging food for holiday outreach projects, or any numerous church service-oriented activities in which schools and districts partner.

A natural outcome of parent participation is a developing relationship with staff at school. Even if parents are not actively engaged in some of the school activities, they still need to make an effort to develop a relationship with the school.

INCREASING PARENT INVOLVEMENT

As educators, we know that student success is enhanced by engaged and supportive parents. Parent involvement is a significant contributor to student success. For many schools, particularly more affluent schools, parent involvement happens almost automatically. The schools don't have to think about it or make any plans to change it. For other schools, particularly low-income schools, parent involvement is an increasing challenge. It is a challenge that we cannot ignore. By engaging in some of the strategies offered in this chapter, and many more to come, school staffs can work together to effectively improve parent involvement.

While every school and community has many common threads, each also has its own unique obstacles. Once parent involvement has been defined, staffs need to identify the barriers that often get in the way of developing a better connection between home and school. As you will see, this is crucial, because identifying barriers helps turn talk into action.

Theory to Practice

 Form a committee to focus on parent involvement or add the topic to an existing committee.

 Define parent involvement.

 Discuss the difference between volunteering and parent involvement.

Key Concepts

1

Barriers and challenges to parent involvement

2

Differentiated parent support

3

Three Tiers

5

The Barriers of Parental Involvement

"Life, misfortunes, isolation, abandonment, poverty, are battlefields which have their heroes; obscure heroes, sometimes greater than the illustrious heroes."

~ Victor Hugo

If we are going to successfully work to increase parent involvement, one of the first things we need to look at is what is keeping parents from being involved. To effectively increase parent involvement, we need first to understand the barriers and then work to remove or reduce them. The range of barriers emphasizes the diversity of our parents. Rather than expecting parents to adapt to us, we need to create a parent involvement system that meets parents' diverse needs. Most schools try the same old strategies year after year to involve parents. We send flyers, newsletters, and emails. This works well for some of our parents. Which parents? The highly functioning, most likely somewhat affluent parents. But what can we do when our strategies are not working for all of our parents? According to Dr. Joyce Epstein, director of the Center on School, Family and Community Partnerships, "I think people are realizing that to develop more diverse and equitable community involvement programs, they need more planning." We cannot continue to just talk about parent involvement, set a goal to increase it, and hope it happens. We know this doesn't work.

The message is very clear: If we are struggling to increase parent involvement, if this is truly a priority and an important goal, we cannot continue to utilize the same practices. Einstein's definition of insanity is doing the same thing over and over and expecting different results. Before we try different practices and strategies, we want to ensure that they will be effective. So we need to start by asking about what it is that stops parents from becoming more involved with their children's education. Is it lack of care? Is it lack of concern? Do they not love their children as much as other parents? Of course they do. The answer is not that simple. The reasons for poor parent involvement are varied and numerous. I am sure you are already familiar with many of them. Some of the most common barriers for effective parent involvement are language, parents' education level, mental health, physical health, and parents' jobs.

Think about it: If you moved to a new country and didn't speak the language, how would you get involved in your child's education? Would you be able to help them with their homework? Would you attend the school events? If you didn't even graduate from high school, would you be comfortable at your child's school? Would you have enough knowledge and skills to help them with their schoolwork? If you were getting by okay without an education, would education be more of a priority for you, or less? For poor mental or physical health — how would you deal with that? Would you have any support from family or friends? Would you have the resources that you need to become healthy? Try for a moment to put yourself in the place of some of your parents. How would you deal with some of the adversity that they are facing?

At Los Pen, we decided to try to gain a greater understanding of what was hindering parents from becoming involved. We strove to uncover what barriers were keeping parents from supporting, participating, and modeling what their children need for their academic success. What we found is that many of our parents were struggling with the barriers mentioned above: language, education level, mental health, physical health, or job schedules. What we also discovered is that many of our most struggling parents shared another barrier. We found that a common thread for parents struggling the most with parent involvement is that many of them are missing basic human needs. They are in survival mode. They may not know where their next meal is coming from or how they are going to pay the rent. They can barely make ends meet, and sometimes can't. If they work, they may work two or three minimum wage jobs. Parents become so overwhelmed that they can't even begin to think about their children's education. In fact, for many, what they value most about school is that it provides a safe and free place for children to spend their day while their parents are at work.

As we continued to study our parents and the barriers that were keeping them from being a helpful part of their children's education, the idea of differentiated parent support was born.

Differentiated Parent Support

We began to realize that what works for one parent does not work for all parents. In our school we have a wide variety of parents, just as we do with our students. As varied as our students' needs are when they walk through the classroom door, so are our parents' needs. It became clear that we need to meet parents where they are to get them where we'd like them to be. Continuing to practice typical strategies such as flyers and newsletters is fine. This is a strategy that will work for many parents, but we can't stop there. The typical strategies cannot be our only strategies. This will only work for a segment of our parents. We began to relate how we work with our students to how we need to work with our parents. We don't treat our students all exactly the same. We can't. They are too diverse. We have learned that if we want success for all students, we have to assess their needs and create an individualized plan for each of them, implement that plan, and then evaluate if it is working.

Have you ever had a classroom of students that are all at the same reading level, math level, and writing level? I doubt it. For years, educators have had to practice "differentiated instruction" with students. We don't have a choice if we want students to be successful.

As a teacher, you would not expect a fourth grade student at a second grade reading level to be able to be successful with a fourth grade reading book. So if we practice differentiated instruction and our results show that it is working, we began to think, why not practice "Differentiated Parent Support"? We know that we can no longer treat all students the same and expect them to be successful. Well the same is true for our parents — we can no longer treat parents all the same and expect successful parent involvement. So out of necessity, the idea of "Differentiated Parent Support" is a system that we created. And our experience is that it can effectively increase parent involvement.

Before we go on, I'd like you to take a moment to think about your own parent community. In the area of parent involvement, try to estimate what percentage of your parents are doing a good job. These are the parents who get their children to school every day and on time. They arrive at school fed, with homework, and ready to learn. You can tell by their progress that someone is working with them at home and supporting and encouraging the importance of school. Next, try to estimate what percentage of your parents are doing an okay job but need to improve. Their children come to school but are sometimes late. They don't consistently have homework done. You suggest areas in which to work with them at home but don't seem to get the parents' cooperation consistently. Finally, try to estimate what percentage of your parents are really struggling and need to dramatically increase their parent involvement. Their children's attendance may be inconsistent. The students' backpacks are filled with papers that are never reviewed by parents. Homework is rarely completed. School just doesn't seem like a priority.

This is what we did at Los Pen. We began to look at our parents as three separate groups, similar to what you might do with a reading or math group. You have the high-achieving readers, the readers at grade level, and the struggling readers. Well, you also have high-achieving parents, average parents, and struggling parents. Based on this thinking, we designed Differentiated Parent Support with three tiers. Tier One families are the parents who are doing a good job. The Tier Two families are the parents who are doing an okay job but need to improve. Tier Three families are the parents who are struggling and who need to increase their parent involvement. After years of practicing Differentiated Parent Support, we actually added a fourth tier. Fortunately, the fourth tier is a small percentage, but they are a reality. They are the parents who, no matter what we do to provide support and encourage involvement, continue to be disengaged and unsupportive of their children's academic success. For this group, we put all of our energy and focus on the students to attempt to neutralize the lack of parent support the children are receiving at home.

While every family is very unique and individual, there are enough similarities to group them into these tiers. As with students, we could probably create several more tiers, but we decided to stay with four to help to make the system more practical and manageable.

Los Pen's Differentiated Parent Support tiers typically divide into the following percentages:

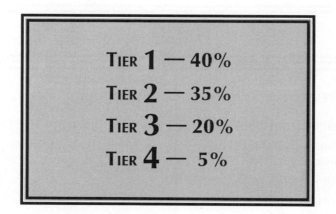

Tier **1** — 40%

Tier **2** — 35%

Tier **3** — 20%

Tier **4** — 5%

Once we determined the tiers, we needed to determine the best way to support each group of parents. Just as with our students, to reach parents at different levels, we have to try different strategies and activities. Here is a brief overview of the groups and the activities we use to support them. The tiers and activities to support them are described in greater detail in the following three chapters.

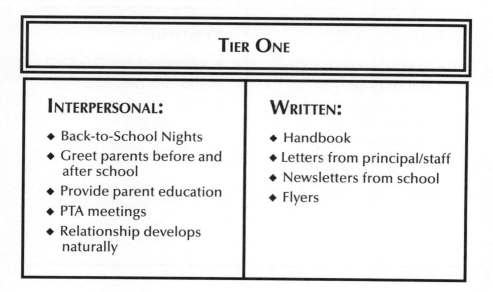

TIER ONE

INTERPERSONAL:

◆ Back-to-School Nights
◆ Greet parents before and after school
◆ Provide parent education
◆ PTA meetings
◆ Relationship develops naturally

WRITTEN:

◆ Handbook
◆ Letters from principal/staff
◆ Newsletters from school
◆ Flyers

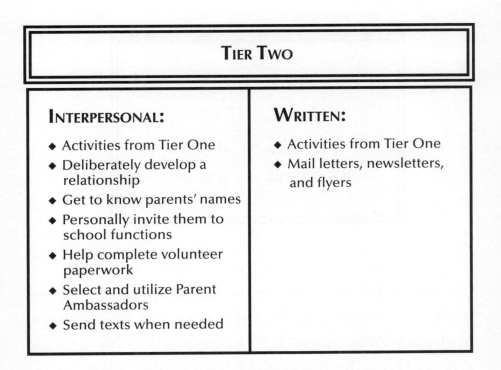

TIER TWO

INTERPERSONAL:

- Activities from Tier One
- Deliberately develop a relationship
- Get to know parents' names
- Personally invite them to school functions
- Help complete volunteer paperwork
- Select and utilize Parent Ambassadors
- Send texts when needed

WRITTEN:

- Activities from Tier One
- Mail letters, newsletters, and flyers

TIER THREE

INTERPERSONAL:

- Activities from Tier One and Tier Two
- Relationship, relationship, relationship
- Home visits
- Call parents with "good news"
- Resources for basic family needs
- Transportation

WRITTEN:

- Activities from Tier One and Tier Two
- Frequent, handwritten notes home

To identify parents and determine which tier they fall into, we use input from staff and the experiences we have with the families. We also developed a questionnaire that can help assess which tier the parents seem to fit into. This is not necessary to complete for every family, just for the families that are new or unknown to the school staff.

We then identify the families in a discreet way on a system that is connected to our student information system. This facilitates our ability to generate labels, phone calls, flyers, or activities specifically for each tier. Just as with students, the goal is to recognize the tier parents are on and then work with them and teach them how they can be more supportive, involved parents. We want to help move parents from Tier Three to Tier Two and ultimately to Tier One, as they learn to support their children in their academic success.

Theory to Practice

 Work with other staff members to determine what barriers and challenges are affecting parent involvement at your school

 Distribute the Differentiated Parent Support Tier Evaluation to staff

 Estimate the percentage of parents in each of the four tiers

Key Concepts

1

Tier One Parents

2

Parent Forum

3

Code of Conduct

6

Tier One:
The Ideal Parent

"The important thing is not so much that every child should be taught, as that every child should be given the wish to learn."

~ John Lubbock

At Los Pen, Tier One is our biggest group of parents. It includes the type of parents who arrive at school, ready, willing, and anxious to be involved. Quite often this group had a very positive personal experience with school and most likely graduated from high school. Many of the parents in Tier One have either graduated or have some college experience. Education is a priority for their children, and they are able to support their children in school.

A Tier One Family: The Smiths have been married for seventeen years. They met in high school. Sue went to college and pursued her teaching credential. Her husband, John, decided to forgo college to pursue his dream of being a professional artist. They settled in a middle-income home near a local elementary school. Both of their daughters attended preschool and both parents worked with them at home to help them learn. They registered their first daughter for kindergarten on the day that registration started and attended the kindergarten orientation. They always take their girls to their first day of school to meet their teachers. The children attend school regularly and have rarely been late. When they arrive at school, they are rested, fed, and ready to learn. Their homework is complete and they have often completed extra tasks. Because of their parents, they know that school is important and that their education is a priority. They take their lessons seriously and enjoy learning. They are a typical Tier One family.

Think of the Huxtables from the television show, The Cosby's.

STRATEGIES FOR TIER ONE, TWO, AND THREE FAMILIES

We created strategies for each of the tiers to support parent involvement. Additional strategies will be shared in greater detail in each of the following chapters describing the tiers. The strategies are like stair steps. The Tier One strategies are provided for every tier. The second tier parents receive the Tier One strategies and also have additional strategies geared to Tier Two families. For Tier Three, all strategies from Tier One and Tier Two are used in addition to some specific strategies geared toward Tier Three families. For Tier Four families, we try every strategy we can think of to encourage their involvement. When we are not successful after numerous attempts, we continue to use all of the strategies, but also increase our focus on the student at school.

One of the universal and most effective strategies for all parents is our NEU Parent Forum.

NEU Parent Forum

At Los Pen we begin the year with a mandatory "No Excuses" parent meeting. We call it the NEU Parent Forum. We initially offer the meeting three times and include a flyer inviting parents to attend one of the forums in the first day packet. In the flyer, we describe it as a "mandatory" meeting. While we can't really enforce it, we tell all parents that they are expected to attend a meeting once during their children's career at Los Pen. At the meetings, we ask every parent who attends to sign in. We enter this information into a data system to generate a list of parents who still need to attend. As you can imagine, the meetings are well attended by our Tier One families—thus we have about 35 percent of the parents attend the initial meetings. We then schedule two more NEU Parent Forums. We create a letter from the principal with the two new dates for the meetings. In the letter, we mention that we know that they weren't able to make it to the first three meetings, but because the meetings are mandatory, we have scheduled several more dates.

Then instead of sending the letters home in backpacks, we personally address the letter to the parents and send it in the mail. It's interesting—there is just something about a letter being sent home

"To the parents of" that seems to get their attention. It also lets parents know that we are keeping good records, and we know that they have yet to attend a meeting. Once again, as you can imagine, not everyone attends the meetings. So we schedule another date. In the event that they still don't attend an NEU Parent Forum, these parents will receive another letter. For this final meeting, we not only send a letter to their home, but the principal and/or counselor make phone calls inviting the parents to attend. During the phone conversation, if parents say they still cannot attend the final meeting, then the principal and counselor offer to schedule an appointment for a home visit to share this important information. That offer usually seems to encourage parents to make it to the final meeting. If parents still do not attend a meeting, a home visit is scheduled. For the home visit, the principal and counselor may go together, or if the teacher would like to go, then one of them makes the visit with the teacher. We never allow anyone to make a home visit alone. If we make a home visit, we cover the same topics that we do at the one-hour meeting. The topics are:

- ✔ Los Pen Pledge
- ✔ Specifics of NEU
- ✔ Attendance
- ✔ Three-Way Pledge
- ✔ Parent Goals
- ✔ Take Five
- ✔ Code of Conduct

Los Pen Pledge: Los Pen has had the same pledge for ten years: "We are committed to creating a school that knows no limits to the academic success of each student." We share the pledge with parents to establish the level of commitment from staff and then ask for the same commitment from parents. We talk about the notion of "No Excuses."

Specifics of NEU: We articulate for parents that NEU is a way to promote college readiness beginning in elementary school. "No Excuses" is a pervading concept throughout the campus. It is an integral part of the culture. This concept applies to all three stakeholders, the student, parent, and the teacher. Beginning with the teachers, the belief is that there are no excuses for students not to be successful.

Attendance: We discuss how critical attendance is to student success. This includes arriving on time. As part of our conversation, we talk about "soft truancy." Soft truancy is keeping children home for reasons other than illness or bereavement. While truancy is a harsh word, it is important for parents to know how serious it is that students are in school every day ready to learn. We actually share our school attendance data. We display the days of the week, Monday through Friday, and using a bar graph show the amount of absences. I think it is probably no surprise to you that Monday and Friday have the highest rates of absences. We then translate that to the amount of time that has been lost to learning. We start with days, then hours, then minutes. As you can see on the chart below, that is a LOT of time lost!

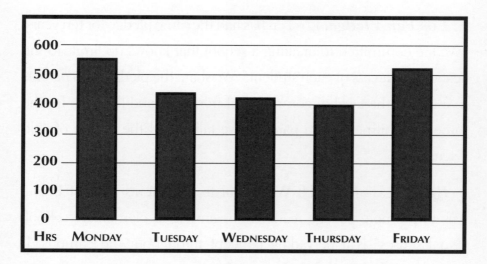

INSTRUCTIONAL HOURS MISSED ON MONDAYS VS THURSDAYS

Los Pen Students Collectively Miss An Additional
152 Days of Instructional Time
912 Hours of Instructional Time
54,720 Minutes of Instructional Time
Mondays versus Thursdays

We then share the attendance data of our highest performing school. Again, I am sure you will not be surprised to know that this is also the school with the lowest rate of absences. The last point we make about attendance is the correlation of "hard truancy" in middle and high school and the knowledge that "hard truancy" starts with "soft truancy." Soft truancy sends the message that school is not a priority and that it is okay to miss it when it isn't convenient. This is not the message that we want to send to our children.

THREE-WAY PLEDGE

Along with many of our NEU schools across the country, we ask for parents to participate in a three-way pledge. The pledge includes parents, students, and teachers. The pledge is a way to formally and purposefully make a commitment to their children's success. We share the pledge with parents at the NEU Parent Forum and then ask them to sign it at the fall parent-teacher conference. Take a look at the sample of the Three-Way Pledge below:

NO EXCUSES UNIVERSITY THREE-WAY PLEDGE

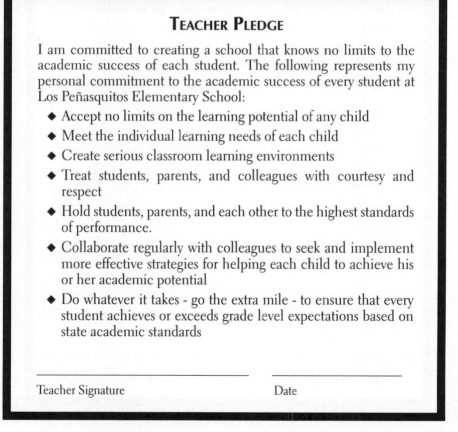

TEACHER PLEDGE

I am committed to creating a school that knows no limits to the academic success of each student. The following represents my personal commitment to the academic success of every student at Los Peñasquitos Elementary School:

- ◆ Accept no limits on the learning potential of any child
- ◆ Meet the individual learning needs of each child
- ◆ Create serious classroom learning environments
- ◆ Treat students, parents, and colleagues with courtesy and respect
- ◆ Hold students, parents, and each other to the highest standards of performance.
- ◆ Collaborate regularly with colleagues to seek and implement more effective strategies for helping each child to achieve his or her academic potential
- ◆ Do whatever it takes - go the extra mile - to ensure that every student achieves or exceeds grade level expectations based on state academic standards

_____   _____
Teacher Signature   Date

No Excuses University Three-Way Pledge

continued

Student Pledge

I understand that my education is very important to my future. It will help me develop the tools I need to become a successful and productive person. I know that my education now will prepare me for college in the future. Because of this I am committed to following the requirements found in my No Excuses University Student Handbook. In addition, I commit to:

◆ Arriving at school every day on time unless I am ill

◆ Following the rules and the six pillars of character of our school

◆ Completing and turning in homework on time every day

◆ Returning letters, corrected work, and other school materials to my parents

_____   _____

Student Signature   Date

Teacher + Student + Parent = Success

No Excuses University Three-Way Pledge

continued

Parent Pledge

I understand that my child's education today is essential for their success in life. This experience will support him/her to become a successful and productive person. It will also prepare them for college if they so choose to attend. Because of this I am committed to following the requirements found in my No Excuses University Parent Handbook. These responsibilities are found in the:

- ◆ Mission, Vision, Shared Commitment, and Goal of Los Peñasquitos
- ◆ Parent Code of Conduct
- ◆ "Take Five" Commitment
- ◆ Parent Goals Commitment
- ◆ Commitment to ensuring my child attends school on time every day unless they are ill

Each of these responsibilities speaks to my commitment to support Los Peñasquitos in order to ensure a bright future for my child.

_____   _____

Parent Signature   Date

TEACHER + STUDENT + PARENT = SUCCESS

Parent Goals

We encourage parents to create and complete parent goals. We talk about the idea that since we expect every student in our school to have a "student goal," we believe that parents can also have goals. This is an excellent strategy for parents to model goal-making with their children. Additionally, it is an opportunity for parents to try and enhance their parenting skills. There are two goals. One is for their children's education. We encourage them to list goals to support their children academically. We suggest that they review their children's student goals and base their academic goals on that. For example, if a child's goal is to increase his or her vocabulary, then the parent could make a goal to read to him or her every night. Or if the goal is to learn multiplication facts, parents could make a goal to help with practicing the times tables every night. The second parent goal is in the area of enhancing parenting skills. This is very individual for each parent. It may be a goal to attend a class, or it could be a goal to spend more quality time with their children. Again, the goals are going to be as varied and diverse as our parents.

"Tell me and I forget. Show me and I remember. Involve me and I understand."

~ Chinese proverb

My Parenting Goals

Supporting Academics:

GOAL:_____

STEPS FOR SUCCESS:

- ◆ _____

- ◆ _____

- ◆ _____

Enhancing Parenting Skills:

GOAL:_____

STEPS FOR SUCCESS:

- ◆ _____

- ◆ _____

- ◆ _____

Take Five

In today's fast-paced world, it has been said that we are losing the "art of dialogue." Dialogue is an important aspect of learning.

In meaningful dialogue, children learn to listen, think, reason, and communicate ideas. The ability to do this enhances academic success. Unfortunately, as our world has had more technological advances and has continued to move at an ever-increasing pace, we are losing the opportunities for dialogue. Think of how children now spend their days, compared to how children spent their days just twenty years ago. Twenty years ago, boys and girls still went out to play with children in their neighborhoods. It was a common guideline for children that they had to come in when the streetlights went on. Playing outside with neighborhood friends helped children to learn to negotiate, compromise, cooperate, and get along. In today's world, there are very few children allowed the same opportunities. Now, playing with friends is arranged or happens during scheduled activities or team sports. When those aren't available, many children are spending their time with technology. They are either watching TV or playing a game attached to a TV or computer. If we want children to learn the art of dialogue, we have to be more purposeful in engaging them in dialogue. Take Five is designed with that in mind.

Take Five is a concept developed to encourage meaningful dialogue between parent and child. It is intended to take no more than five minutes each day, although parents and children can certainly expand that time. The questions are used as a framework to focus on student success. We also provide a magnet to families to keep on their refrigerator as a daily reminder and include the steps in our Parent Handbook. The following is a sample of Take Five:

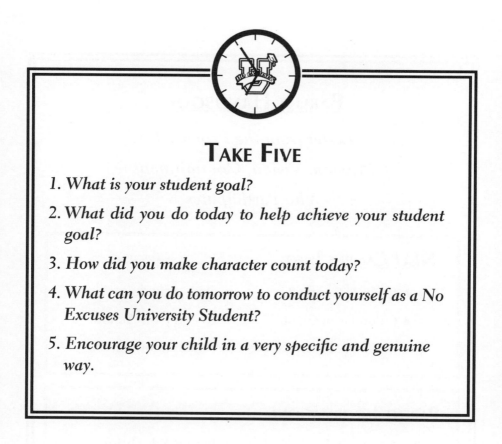

TAKE FIVE

1. *What is your student goal?*

2. *What did you do today to help achieve your student goal?*

3. *How did you make character count today?*

4. *What can you do tomorrow to conduct yourself as a No Excuses University Student?*

5. *Encourage your child in a very specific and genuine way.*

HANDBOOK

At each of the NEU Parent Forums, parents receive a parent handbook. The handbook is a compilation of information that we were already providing to parents throughout the year in a variety of formats. We simply pulled all the information together in more professional way into a Parent Handbook. The contents of the handbook are listed below, and a sample of the complete handbook is included in the appendix.

We also created a handbook for staff and students. Both of these handbooks are described in Chapter Eight.

Parent Handbook

Letter from the Principal

Mission, Vision, Commitment

Who Participates

NEU Campus Info:

- Code of Conduct
- Calendar of Event
- Meeting Student Needs
- Daily Schedule
- To and From School
- Health Information

Parent Information:

- Parent Code of Conduct
- Parent Endorsement
- Resources
- Parent Education
- Volunteer

College Readiness:

- TAKE 5
- Accountability
- Parent Goal
- Student Leadership Opportunities
- A-G College Requirement
- Student Goal
- College Financing

CODE OF CONDUCT

We created a Code of Conduct for students, staff, and parents that we share at the Parent Forum. To support consistency, we made all three codes of conduct very similar, which creates a common language. Having a common language is instrumental in creating a successful school climate for all three stakeholders.

Can you imagine working at a place where the rules change depending on the supervisor you are working with? Wouldn't that be frustrating and confusing? How much of a challenge would it be to find success without knowing the clear expectations and guidelines?

Then why do we do this to children? Why don't we create school-wide behavior expectations? In many schools, teachers have their own ideas and interpretation of behavior expectations of students, how to teach them and how to correct them. As children move from class to class, from teacher to teacher, from grade to grade, they may often find that the rules change. With Mrs. Smith, you can talk while you are walking in the disorderly line to lunch, but with Mrs. Thompson, you had better be completely silent, in a straight line, and keep your hands to yourself. In one class, you can get up and get a drink or sharpen your pencil any time you feel like it, but when you go to another class for reading, you must stay in your seat. How can we expect children to behave when the rules are always changing? How can they follow the rules if they don't know what they are? Children end up getting in trouble today for something that was totally okay to do yesterday. They also may find themselves getting in trouble for something at school that is okay for them to do at home. Home and school may often have different sets of rules, just as your own rules and behavior at home may differ with how you choose to behave at work. Behavior can sometimes be very different between home and school, particularly when it comes to working with children who come to us from poverty. Schools are middle-class organizations, and the rules often differ with what students have learned at home or with what is acceptable to do at home. We are not talking about right versus wrong; we are talking about "different."

For parents, the same type of confusion can happen. Until we introduce, explain, or teach the expectations for parent behavior and involvement, some parents may not actually know what to do.

To create the most effective school climate system, schools need to begin by creating a common language on which to base behavior expectations. This provides simplicity and consistency. This system needs to be openly shared with parents, so that the entire school community—students, staff, and parents—can be committed to implementing and supporting this common language and the school-wide behavior expectations that are based on this common language. The expectations can be developed into a Code of Conduct. There needs to be a Code of Conduct, not just for the students, but also for all stakeholders in the school community. The three stakeholders in a school community are the student, the staff, and the parents.

When the Los Pen School Climate Committee members returned from a Character Counts! training session, we decided to work together to further enhance our School Climate system, beginning with creating a Code of Conduct based on a common language: the language of character.

Los Pen's Code of Conduct — The Character Pledge

So how do you choose which character traits are most important to use in a Code of Conduct? For the Los Pen staff, this was simple. In 2004, members of the School Climate committee were trained in the six traits of Character Counts. It just so happens that Character Counts is one of the most popular character programs in the country. Created by Michael Josephson, Character Counts is a character program focusing on six character traits, which are referred to as pillars. They are six of the most common and broad-ranging traits. The six traits are Trustworthiness, Respect, Responsibility, Fairness, Caring, and Citizenship. Character Counts offers training and consulting services along with numerous support materials. At its website, you can find oodles of resources such as lesson plans, posters, workbooks, plays, music, stickers, pencils, and much, much more. For more detailed information about Character Counts, visit www.charactercounts.org.

TRUSTWORTHINESS

RESPECT

RESPONSIBILITY

FAIRNESS

CARING

CITIZENSHIP

You may choose to select your own traits to develop your Code of Conduct or you could consider adopting an established character program. A simple search on the Internet brings up a variety of character programs, such as Wise Skills, Project Wisdom, and Life Skills 4 Kids.

So how do you go about establishing this Code of Conduct? How do you select the character traits or behavior expectations? For something this universal and overarching, collaboration is vital. Stakeholders need to feel empowered by being part of the process. Begin by creating a School Climate committee. Strive to include a staff member from every grade level. Committee members need to determine the most important values, beliefs, and principles for their school community. Connect these beliefs, values, and principles to character traits. Select the most critical character traits, and once you have selected your critical traits, develop the specific traits into your Code of Conduct. There are many traits to choose from, but strive to limit your list to four to six traits. A larger list of traits will become too overwhelming and confusing. At this point, take the time to research and review the character programs that are available. It is very likely that you will be able to connect you critical character traits to programs like Character Counts that are already established.

Take the time to ensure that any choice or behavior a student may make relates back to one or more of the traits. For example, if students choose to participate in name-calling, they are not being respectful or caring. If they don't complete their schoolwork or homework, they are not being responsible or trustworthy. Rather than having a long laundry list of school rules, the character traits become your school rules and relate back to the character traits. Since we have adopted our Code of Conduct based on the six pillars of character in Character Counts, our experience at Los Pen is that we can always make a connection to one of the six pillars.

When I arrived at Los Pen, there was a ten-page rule handbook. As I worked with students, I began to realize that many of the students truly didn't know all of the rules. I was able to determine this by simply asking, "What is your understanding of the rule for .....?" You can fill in the blank with hallway behavior, bathroom behavior, playground behavior, equipment use, etc. You may be very surprised to discover that their perception is very different than the expectations of the staff. If students don't have a clear understanding of the rules and the behavior expectations, they will not be successful in following them. I began checking with teachers. Guess what I found? There were many teachers who also didn't know the rules that were written in the handbook. I found that different teachers had different understandings of the rules! There was not enough consistency and plenty of room for confusion.

Now add to this the confusion that many children have arrived at school with a very different set of rules — home rules versus school rules. A perfect example of this is the rule of self-defense. Have you ever heard a student say, "Well my mom told me that if anyone hits me or pushes me, that I can hit them or push them back"? Is it possible that a parent today still provides that guidance? You betcha. Check it out for yourself. Hold a discussion about self-defense with a classroom of students. Let them know that honesty is most important and that no one will be in trouble for whatever they answer. Then ask, "How many of your parents tell you that it is okay to hit someone if they hit you first?" Every year, in my very informal research at Los Pen, I have discovered that more than 50 percent of the students will raise their hands. Of course the problem is that if they follow their parents' advice, they will be getting in trouble at school because the rules at school are different. At school, it is unacceptable to resort to violence even if someone strikes first. It is clear that we must explicitly teach students the rules if we want them to follow them.

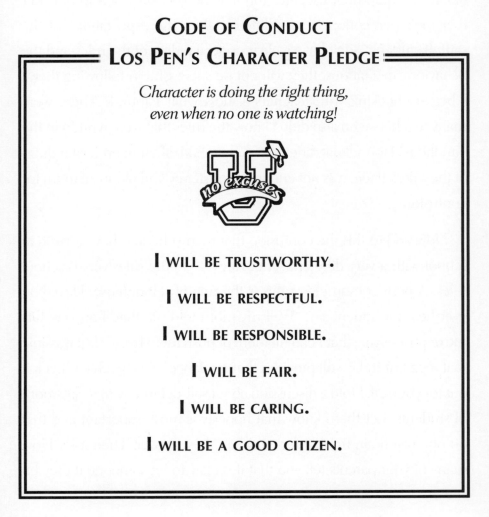

CODE OF CONDUCT
LOS PEN'S CHARACTER PLEDGE

Character is doing the right thing,
even when no one is watching!

I WILL BE TRUSTWORTHY.

I WILL BE RESPECTFUL.

I WILL BE RESPONSIBLE.

I WILL BE FAIR.

I WILL BE CARING.

I WILL BE A GOOD CITIZEN.

After we established the Code of Conduct, we created procedures and guidelines to teach the students the behavior expectations. In the beginning of every school year, teachers review the Code of Conduct with their students. Every teacher leads classroom discussions about each character trait that is part of the Code of Conduct. Once each of the traits is covered, students and teachers sign a laminated poster of the Code of Conduct. This serves as a promise and commitment to follow the Code of Conduct. Each classroom teacher then displays the Code of Conduct poster prominently in the classroom as a daily visual reminder.

A copy of each classroom's signed Code of Conduct is kept in a binder in the office. If a student is sent to the office for discipline incidents, the copy of his or her classroom's poster is another visual reminder of the commitment to follow the Code of Conduct. This can be utilized during the discussion about behavior.

After teachers have taught the Code of Conduct to their students, reinforce the expectations with a Code of Conduct assembly. At Los Pen, the principal and counselor facilitate these assemblies. Grade levels meet in the Multipurpose Room for approximately twenty minutes. The assembly needs to be held within the first two weeks of school. Since the Code of Conduct has already been reviewed in the classroom, this assembly is to reinforce the message and emphasize the priority of behavior expectations.

To support the common language and create clarity and consistency, connect rewards and discipline documents to the Code of Conduct. Instead of having a "Caught You Being Good Award," turn it into a Character Award. Instead of a discipline referral, make it a Character Violation.

LOS PEÑASQUITOS
CODE OF CONDUCT
CHARACTER VIOLATION

*Character is doing the right thing,
even when no one is watching!*

Student Name: _____

Date _____

☐ Classroom   ☐ Outside

Violation of the following character trait:

☐ Trustworthiness
☐ Responsibility
☐ Respect
☐ Fairness
☐ Caring
☐ Citizenship

Explanation: _____

_____

_____

_____

Staff Member: _____

Student Signature: _____

Parent Signature: _____

Make everything connect to the common language of character. This consistency increases the likelihood of students being successful and following the rules. The language of character becomes a big part of the school culture and climate. When the staff begins to utilize the common language, students hear the same messages from everyone. Standards and behavior expectations become very clear, empowering students to make the right choices and to accept responsibility and consequences when they make a mistake. Having a Code of Conduct based on the same traits for staff and parents provides even more consistency, which supports success for all students.

The transition to this common language can be fairly easy. Once you have created a school climate based on the common language of character, support this code of conduct with handbooks, behavior plans, and training for all three stakeholders, including parents. There is no need to reinvent the wheel. Take a look at your current documents and find ways to align them with your new Code of Conduct. The Code of Conduct for parents is first introduced in the Parent Forum and is included in the Parent Handbook.

Some of the strategies described to use for our Tier One parents in this chapter are fairly common strategies that some schools may already be using. One of the most effective strategies to enhance parent involvement is the "mandatory" Parent Forum. Not only are we able to introduce helpful concepts, we are also able to clearly establish expectations. Information shared at this meeting becomes a foundational piece of parent involvement. Referring to it as "mandatory," holding it in the beginning of the year, and using our multileveled approach to communicate to parents about the forum works very well to get the majority of parents to one of the meetings. All of the strategies utilized for Tier One parents are also used for Tier Two, Three, and Four parents. As you will see in the following chapters, we use supplementary strategies for each of the added tiers.

Theory to Practice

 Begin to plan a parent forum. Who will facilitate the meetings? How many will you have? What system will you use to keep track of attendance?

 Discuss creating a Three-Way Pledge with staff. Decide if this is a strategy that you would like to utilize. If so, create your school's Three-Way Pledge.

Think about creating a Parent Handbook. What would you include in the handbook?

Key Concepts

1

Tier Two Parents

2

Parent Education

7

Tier Two:
The Inconsistent Parent

"The best inheritance a parent can give to his children is a few minutes of their time each day."

~ M. Grundler

The next tier is our Tier Two parent. For Los Pen, this group is usually a smaller group than our Tier One parents. These parents may want their children to be successful but don't quite know how to support them. Perhaps they perceive that they don't have the authority to expect their children to do well in school because they may not have been very successful themselves. High school graduation may not have been one of their life experiences, and they may not have the confidence to push and encourage their children. They may be dealing with life challenges and demands and struggling to find a balance. Education may be important but lower on their list of priorities. There are other things going on in their lives that have a greater priority.

A Tier Two Family: Barbara is a single mom with three boys. She lives in the section 8 apartments across the street from the school. These are the same apartments that she grew up in, and her mom still lives nearby. Barbara never graduated from high school and is limited in what kind of job she can qualify for. She receives some government assistance, but would really like to work. Yet in order for her to take care of her children, she would need a job making enough money to pay for childcare. With her lack of education and training, this is just not realistic. So she decides to try to find a job within the school system so that her schedule matches her children and she won't have to pay for childcare. She applies for a job at the school as a yard duty. She is modeling working for her children, although it is an entry-level position. Realizing the value of education, she encourages her children to work hard in school and to make good behavior choices so that they can graduate from high school. But there is very little discussion about college and future career choices. With all of the stress of being a single mom and making ends meet, the children don't receive as much help at home as they need. Papers are returned most of the time, and she attempts to make it to as many school events as she can. They don't own a car, so they stay very close to home within in the neighborhood. Things are so tight that if they didn't receive support from the community, they would not experience much holiday cheer. They are also grateful for monthly groceries and free bread on Fridays.

Think of the Connors from the television show Roseanne.

STRATEGIES FOR TIER TWO FAMILIES

Tier Two parents are parents who are inconsistently involved. They have a desire to support their children, they believe education is important, but they may not have the time, skills, or capacity. They are struggling with some barriers that are keeping them from being more involved.

All Tier One activities are used with Tier Two parents, with the addition of several other strategies to differentiate support. Some of the strategies are fairly simple — as simple as putting important information in an envelope, addressing it to "The parents of," placing a stamp on it, and putting it in the U.S. Mail. Somehow parents seem to view a letter addressed to them more importantly than a flyer in a backpack. Just think about when you receive junk mail. Do you read it all? Most people don't, but we almost always read the mail that is addressed to us and looks official. So when there are events such as back to school nights, parent-teacher conferences, and open house, mail the announcement to all of your Level Two and Level Three parents. While it is a small added expense, the results are worth it.

Communicating with Tier Two and Tier Three parents can often be a bit frustrating. More and more, folks no longer have a house line. Their primary phones are cell phones. How many times have you attempted to contact Level Two or Level Three parents whose cell phones don't accept voicemails, or who have full voice mailboxes?

Well, here is another fairly simple strategy: Text them! I promise you that almost every single parent will respond to a text message. Sending text messages has become a very common form of communication for many people, particularly younger generations. Many of our parents are in a generation that has had cell phones around since they were born. Because they have grown up with the technology of cell phones and the ability to send text messages, it is a familiar and thus comfortable form of communication for them. The easiest way to text parents is to have a prepaid cell phone for office use. This avoids the concern of personal cell phone numbers becoming public. There is also an option on most phone services to block your phone number when making an outgoing phone call. The text message can be brief. Simply send a text to call the school and include the number to call or send a text message about the day and time of an important event.

Another technology that can be utilized is email. While not everyone has a computer and email, it is becoming more and more common. For those who do have the technology, email is a great method of communication. Many schools and districts use automated dialing systems to reach out to the entire school community to notify families of school events and emergencies. Many of these systems also have an option to send an email. So emails can be sent automatically to all families.

A note of caution: Use text messages, automated dialing, and automated emails sparingly. If the frequency is too high, the message will be treated like many people treat junk mail, and the message will be ignored. I think an effective general guideline is to limit the use of these strategies to no more than twice a month.

Another common thread with Tier Two and Tier Three parents is a lack of parenting skills. How often have you worked with a child, only to discover that his or her behavior is a result of poor structure or lack of teaching at home? This is one of the reasons why I think providing parent education is vital.

Parent Education

Parenting is one of the most challenging jobs with the least amount of training! Think about it: You get instructions and manuals for almost everything—cell phones, coffee makers, stereos, cars. What kind of manual did you receive with your child? Any directions? The only thing that we get with our children is a piece of paper called a birth certificate. And at the bottom is a no return, no refunds, no exchanges policy. Then we proceed to parent either the way we were parented or the opposite of the way we were parented because we hated what our parents did. Add to that the other parent and his or her ideas for parenting, and we've got a big problem on our hands.

Why don't we offer more parent education? For one, it's extra work. Two, we don't always get the attendance we would like, and three, many of the parents that we would most like to reach never make the effort to attend.

In spite of the reasons, we need to provide opportunities to support parents and help them to expand their knowledge of parenting. This can be accomplished at PTA meetings, school meetings, back to school nights, parent workshops, newsletters, conferences, and individual consultations. There are many topics available that can be facilitated by any willing staff or community member. Teachers, counselors, principals, police officers, parent facilitators, or other community members can facilitate parenting classes. There are many local agencies that offer presentations for free. You just have to find them and request their services.

Providing parent education is a valuable component of increasing parent involvement. To increase interest and generate better attendance, rather than labeling it parent education, create a name that is more positive and catchy, such as "Parent University." This reduces the possibility of negative stigmas and helps to enhance the perception of parent education. During our NEU Parent Forum discussed in Chapter Five, we talk about Parent University. One of the things we share with parents is, "Hey, think of it like this, you already have your high school diploma — you have a child. Now work on your associate's, bachelor's, master's or Ph.D. by participating in some courses to enhance your parenting skills."

Schedule classes as far as possible in advance. Ideally, it is best to provide parent education dates at the very beginning of the year. As dates get closer, include them in the newsletter and on the marquee, and send out flyers. One of our NEU schools, Vermont Elementary School in San Bernardino, actually created an NEU Extensions Course catalogue. Modeled after a college course catalogue, it lists all courses for the year with a description, cost, and how to register. A sample of this innovative idea is in the appendix.

So how can you decide on topics? And how do you create the presentations? Well, a great way to decide on topics is to survey parents. Find out what they are interested in learning about. Or survey the staff. Find out what areas the students seem to be struggling with the most and offer classes in that area. After deciding on topics, you can either purchase curriculum or create your own presentations.

There is some exceptional parent education curriculum available that is set and ready to go, such as Developing Capable Young People, Positive Discipline, Redirecting Children's Behavior, and Active Parenting of Teens. These are all excellent programs. They come with facilitator guides, workbooks, and sometimes DVDs and tapes. Many of these programs also provide training for facilitators. In fact, some of them actually require facilitator training and certification. The only downside to the facilitator training is the time and money for the actual training. If you have the time and money, I suggest that it is worth it to invest in some of these programs. But if you don't have the time and money, that is still no excuse to not offer parenting education. Go to the local bookstore or the Internet, and check out the myriad of books written by parenting experts, such as *How to Talk So Kids Will Listen, Ending Homework Hassles, Sibling Rivalry,* and *Raising Self-Reliant Children In a Self-Indulgent World*. Find a willing facilitator to read the books and to create a synopsis or brief overview. These cliff notes can then be turned into PowerPoint presentations that can be delivered in a two-hour meeting. While you won't be able to provide all of the details of the book, at least parents can hear some of the overarching concepts and ideas from the author. It is not likely that many of these parents in Tier Two and Tier Three will ever purchase and read some of these books. Many parents are dealing with barriers and challenges. They may not have the time to read, or they may not be able to read at such a level. At many schools, we are working with parents who are not able to read due to language. If you choose to create a PowerPoint from books, just be sure to reference the author and book. It's also a great idea to have a few books available for purchase at the presentation. The school can even purchase the books and give them out via a drawing, which also becomes an incentive for parents to attend future trainings. Once parents have heard a general overview of the ideas, strategies, and concepts in the books, they are much more likely to make the time to read them if they have the ability.

POSSIBLE TOPICS

There are many potential topics that can be created and presented as a PowerPoint. Here are some examples of some of the topics that have been created and presented at Los Pen.

Home to School Connection: Connecting 4 Success

Based on books like John Rosemund's *Ending Homework Hassles*, this session focuses on ways to help parents create positive relationships with their children's school to enhance the home and school partnership. There are ideas for parents on how to prepare for their children's school conference and how to participate in the conference. This session also addresses ways for parents to support children in the area of homework. There are ideas on how to set up a homework space and how to create a successful homework schedule.

Managing Your Child's Behavior: The Mistaken Goals of Misbehavior

Information from *Redirecting Children's Behavior* by Kathryn Kvols is part of this PowerPoint. This course introduces the concept that all behavior is a form of communication. The idea that when children misbehave it is because they are discouraged is presented. And the four mistaken goals are established and explained to help parents better understand the motivation behind their children's misbehavior so that they may manage it more effectively.

Communicating with Your Child

Primarily from H. Stephen Glenn's work *Developing Capable Young People* and also from Adele Faber's book *How to Talk So Kids Will Listen and Listen So Kids Will Talk*, this presentation focuses on how parents can try to communicate effectively with their children at an early age, which will help parents navigate the more challenging teen years. It also serves as a great introduction and preview of the five-week course "Developing Capable Young People" that is offered later in the year.

Developing Responsibility and Consequences

Highlighting information from H. Stephen Glenn's *Raising Self-Reliant Children in a Self-Indulgent World* and Jane Nelsen's *Positive Discipline*, this presentation focuses on strategies to promote responsibility in children. From assigning chores at home to allowing children to experience consequences, this helps parents establish routines and structure that builds responsibility. This session also introduces the difference in natural versus logical consequences. The four "R's" that make the consequences logical are explored: Consequences need to be related, reasonable, respectful, and revealed. The importance of providing consequences is related to developing responsibility. During the presentation, time is provided so that parents can practice creating some consequences for their own children.

Sibling Rivalry

This presentation was a special request by a Los Pen parent and was very well attended. This PowerPoint presentation is based on the book *Siblings without Rivalry* by Adele Faber and Elaine Mazlish. The authors provide the definition and causes of sibling rivalry and then present strategies that parents can use to deal with sibling rivalry.

Developing Capable Young People Workshop Series

Created by H. Stephen Glenn, the author of *Raising Self-Reliant Children in a Self-Indulgent World,* this is a ten-week workshop that has an exceptional facilitator curriculum, participant notebooks, and DVDs. This workshop equips parents with skills and strategies to maximize their children's potential. Developing Capable Young People introduces participants to the three perceptions and four skills that help to create capable young people. The three perceptions and four skills are:

PERCEPTIONS OF CAPABILITIES

*"I am capable of facing problems and challenges
and gaining strength and wisdom through experience."*

PERCEPTIONS OF SIGNIFICANCE

*"My life has meaning and purpose—who I am
and what I have to offer is of value in the scheme of things."*

PERCEPTIONS OF INFLUENCE

"My actions and choices influence what happens."

INTRAPERSONAL SKILLS

*The tools to respond to feelings effectively, specifically,
self-assessment, self-control and self-discipline.*

INTERPERSONAL SKILLS

*The tools to communicate, cooperate, negotiate,
share, empathize, resolve conflicts,
and listen effectively when dealing with people.*

SYSTEMIC SKILLS

*The tools of responsibility, adaptability,
and flexibility necessary to deal with the environmental family,
social, legal, and other systems in which we live.*

JUDGMENT SKILLS

*The tools to set goals and/or make decisions, judgments,
and choices based on moral
and ethical principles, wisdom, and experience.*

Additional parent education is offered through Parent Information Nights. A guest speaker from the police department or another community agency often presents these events. On these evenings, some examples of topics that may be covered are Alcohol and Drug Awareness, Internet Safety, Stranger Danger, Weapon Awareness, and Domestic Violence. Frequently, these topics are presented where the families live, using a community or meeting room at the apartment complex.

These are just a few of the ideas and topics that we have used at Los Pen. When it comes to parent education, the topics are almost limitless. Last time I went to Amazon.com and searched for "parenting books," there were 57,308 results!! While they may not all be great books, I think that with more than 57,000 options, anyone could find five or six books they value and would like to share with parents to enhance parenting skills and ultimately parent involvement.

Theory to Practice

 Research getting a cell phone for the office

 Create and distribute a parent survey for interest in parent education topics

 Determine who can be facilitators for parent education

Key Concepts

1

Tier Three Parents

2

Strategies

3

Build Relationships

8

Tier Three:
The Struggling Parent

"Too often we underestimate the power of a touch, a smile, a kind word, a listening ear, an honest compliment, or the smallest act of caring, all of which have the potential to turn a life around."

~ Leo Buscaglia

Do you like to use flyers and newsletters to communicate with your parents? If so, don't use just that form of communication with Tier Three parents — it doesn't always work. To be candid, communicating with these adults is a tremendous challenge. Some of these folks never even step foot on your school campus, and it could be months before you ever meet them face-to-face. Their children have learned at an early age that they are dependent on themselves for nearly everything. They wake up, get dressed, and get themselves to school on their own. Homework may be entirely the students' responsibility. Phone calls to these parents may not be returned, and in many cases, you may not even have the correct phone number. Paperwork from the school is rarely read and almost never returned in a timely manner. Their children's attendance is not always good, and it often appears that school is not a priority.

What's going on with these parents? Don't they care about their children? While I realize that this sentiment is pervasive among educators, and at times I have even joined in on this belief, I am reminded of the need to resist such apathy. In most cases, it is an unfair perception, and in many cases, it is an inaccurate one. If we take the time to learn about the family, to really get to know their situation, we often find that they are in survival mode. They worry about paying the rent or feeding their children. They may be unemployed and lack any kind of financial stability, much less health care or any other kind of insurance. You might find that there are issues creating added stress and strain to an already difficult situation. Not all of these parents are "deadbeats" or "drug addicts" as some may suggest, but a small percentage may very well be struggling with substance abuse, mental or physical heath issues, or negative relationships within their homes. With issues like these to worry about, the last thing that comes to their mind for these parents is homework or supporting their children in school. And who could blame them? They just don't have the time, energy, or focus to do it. The challenges that they are dealing with are simply more difficult and time consuming to be concerned about than the education of their children.

*A **Tier Three Family**:* Candice and Jasmine live with their great-grandmother Edith because their mother is in prison and their father is a man they have never met. Though Edith was old enough to retire when she became the official guardian of the girls, she continued to work out of necessity in order to support them. She struggles to make ends meet and picks up her great-granddaughters from childcare exhausted every evening. She barely has the energy to get them home, fed, and in bed at a decent time. The girls routinely arrive at school tired and without homework. Their home life lacks structure and routines. They are often allowed to go to bed with the TV on, and the words "bed time" are not in their vocabulary. Candice, the oldest daughter, is behind in school. There are some terrific after-school interventions that are being offered for her, but her great-grandmother cannot or chooses not to take off from work in order to meet with the school staff about these options. As a result, Candice is becoming very discouraged about school and is now refusing to get dressed for school. All of this, and she is only in the third grade. These habits are now being picked up by her first grade sister. Both girls are falling behind as they have learned that the first rule in their home is "Do whatever you want to do." Much like the Bundy family on television's Married With Children, everyone looks out for "number one," while accountability and personal responsibility is nowhere to be found.

STRATEGIES FOR TIER THREE FAMILIES

Tier Three families are some of the toughest to reach. All of the programs, strategies, and forms of communication we use for our Tier One and Tier Two families should also be used with our Tier Three families. In addition, it is critical that you include a few more. With each additional strategy, it all comes down to *relationship, relationship, relationship!* Initiating and establishing a relationship with Tier Three families is vital. To determine what the barriers and challenges are, you need to have a relationship so that families feel comfortable enough to disclose their greatest challenges. What is keeping them from supporting their children in school? What roadblocks are making their daily relationship with their children a challenge? What can the school do to connect in a way that supports parents' basic needs, and leads to a more stable relationship with their children? In a nutshell, it's all about outreach.

Engagement is a critical element in the outreach efforts between schools and homes. Effective outreach at schools is non-judgmental and has no strings attached. It is about reaching out to families in need to engage them in their children's school success. It is about accepting and loving them while also teaching them how to become better parents and partners in their children's education. Community outreach provides steps and support to enrich and improve their lives and the lives of their children. For many families in poverty, outreach may often be their only means of putting food on the table, a roof over their heads, and clothing on their backs. Basic human needs must be met first, in order for families to successfully engage. This is exactly what *outreach* does.

With outreach as the heart of a new action plan for supporting parents, here are some terrific ways that you can support your Tier Three families.

Home Visits: When parents are unlikely to visit school or to attend school activities, a great way to initiate a relationship is to schedule a home visit. Who should make the home visits? Ideally, the current classroom teacher and another staff member. Even if the teacher is unavailable or unwilling to make a home visit, the principal, counselor, social worker, assistant principal, or health attendant can still accomplish an effective visit. All home visits should be attended by at least two representatives from the school. Schedule the home visits in advance if possible. If parents are reluctant to invite you in their homes or apartments, ask to sit down with them outside on the porch. Show up at a time when you think they may be home, and just casually connect at the front door. The focus here is to initiate a connection. Home visits will not solve all of the issues in the family, but much like the act of parents greeting you at the entrance to their homes, these visits open the door to develop a deeper partnership between the school and the parent.

Free Childcare: Another helpful strategy is to allow parents to bring their children to school events. Many families may not have access to family or friends or the money to pay for a sitter. Therefore, if we want to encourage all parents to attend important events, then we need to provide childcare. If there is funding, provide childcare at the school site. Open up the auditorium or a large assembly area and show a children's movie. Or create engaging activities for different age groups with art or other academic games, or even support children with homework and read with them. If children aren't invited and parents can't arrange childcare, the parents most certainly will not attend the event. If our desire is to try and increase attendance of parents at an event, this is a strategy that we must implement.

Interactive Events: When planning parent events at school, it is important to consider the format and environment. Making the events as welcoming and inviting as possible is very important. Try to provide programs that are less formal and a bit more casual. Rather than having someone up in front of an audience speaking all evening, create events that are more interactive. Allow parents to participate in ways that are comfortable, where anxiety is kept at a minimum. Having a non-English speaking parent come in front of a large crowd to participate in an activity that requires them to speak will spark insecurity and discourage further participation on the part of that parent. Instead, you may want to use a format where you set up an auditorium or library with a variety of activities with information at lots of different tables around the room. Have staff members available at each location to talk with parents one on one or in small groups.

It Doesn't Always Have to Be Academic: Holding fun, social events is a great way to get some of our Tier Three families involved. The events don't need to be expensive or elaborate, like a school carnival or fall festival. They can be simple. Host a family movie night on a big screen in the auditorium. Invite families to bring snacks and blankets to watch Monday Night Football on an outdoor screen at night in the fall. Work with local restaurants to host pizza or ice cream nights for no particular reason other than to build a sense of community. The idea for hosting a social event for families is only limited by the imagination of the people planning it.

Parent Ambassador Program: While the idea of social, fun events is worthwhile, schools also have a number of other events that are essential for parents to attend to support school success for their children. Events such as back to school nights, parent-teacher conferences, open house, and parent forums engage parents in a very meaningful way. So how do we get hard-to-reach, challenging parents to attend?

An innovative way to engage those hard-to-reach parents is through other parents. Parent-to-parent or peer-to-peer communication can be tremendously successful, particularly when we are dealing with language barriers. Recruit and invite some parents to become Parent Ambassadors. Provide training and support to the Parent Ambassadors by creating and sharing guidelines regarding how they can support new families to the school community. Parent Ambassadors make an initial call to new families to share important information about the school and also to begin to establish a mentor-like relationship. During this initial call, the Parent Ambassadors offer their phone numbers and encourage the new families to contact them with any questions. Throughout the year, the Parent Ambassadors contact families to remind them of any important events. To maintain the relationship between families and the Parent Ambassadors, the Ambassadors contact their list of parents on a monthly basis to ensure the family is settling in to their new school community. It is most effective to have an Ambassador to represent every language spoken in your school. For some schools, like Los Pen, that have a myriad of different languages, it may be very, very difficult to have a Parent Ambassador for every language. Don't allow that to be an excuse for not starting a Parent Ambassador program! Just start small and let it grow.

So how can schools connect new parents with a Parent Ambassador and also maintain confidentiality? Well frequently, if parents are given the Parent Ambassador number, many of them may not make the phone call. Why? It's hard to say, but maybe parents are shy, unsure, or overwhelmed. So the more effective option is to give the new parents the phone number to the ambassador parents and they can then initiate contact. To ensure contact between the Parent Ambassadors and new families, while still maintaining confidentiality, there is a simple step that can be taken. When new parents enroll students in the school office, include a Parent Ambassador form as part of the paperwork. The Parent Ambassador form has contact information for new families and is given to the assigned Parent Ambassador.

PARENT AMBASSADOR PROGRAM

Please provide your contact information so that a Parent Ambassador may contact you to share school information and support.

Parent Name: _____

Student Name: _____

Phone Number: _____

Email: _____

The Parent Ambassadors program is one strategy to help connect new families to schools. An even simpler strategy is school directories. Many schools across the country create and provide a school directory. Frequently, this is accomplished with the help of the school PTA. Within the school directory, families are usually listed by the classroom teacher. To take it a step further, some schools also include native language information with each entry so that parents can more easily connect to other parents who share their language.

Virtual Visits: When all else fails, if you can't get them to come to you, then go to them. As mentioned earlier, make home visits. Another option is to create DVDs with important parent information and send the DVDs home for parents to view. A great example takes place at San Jacinto Elementary in Amarillo, Texas, which holds a yearly Parent Forum just like many NEU schools. For parents who do not attend the Forum after several attempts to invite them, San Jacinto sends home a DVD from the principal, Doug Curry. The DVD includes all of the most vital information that parents need to hear. This DVD does not have to be professionally done, just short, simple, and to the point.

While some Tier Three parents can be very challenging to work with, when you are able to find ways to increase their involvement, it is very, very rewarding. Their increased participation translates into more support for their children, which ultimately enhances their opportunity for school and life success.

Theory to Practice

 Identify one Tier Three parent and begin to make a connection with them.

 Evaluate current programs to ensure they are friendly and supportive to Tier Three parents.

 Discuss the possibility of implementing a Parent Ambassador program.

Key Concepts

1

Tier Four Parents

2

Focus on the student

9

Tier Four: The Checked-Out Parent

"Parents have become so convinced that educators know what is best for their children that they forget that they themselves are really the experts."

~ Marian Wright Edelman

Tier Four is typically the smallest and most challenging group of parents. With Tier Four parents, we try every means of engagement and support, but none of it seems to make much of a difference. It's as if we keep hitting a brick wall. While we can continue to invite, encourage, and support, we need to accept the fact that we may not be able to get this parent involved or connected. Our most effective strategy with Tier Four parents is to increase the energy and focus on the students who have Tier Four parents, and to do whatever we can to neutralize the lack of parent involvement while they are with us during the school day. In many ways, we are trying to decrease the negative influences that these parents place on their students. It sounds contrary to what this book is about, but just think about the challenges that these kids bring to school with them. Think of the burden that is placed on their shoulders that distracts them from focusing on their learning. If we can offer a safe haven to these kids, even if only for six to eight hours, then we have made a positive impact that has the potential to change their lives in the long run.

A Tier Four Family

Mackenzie and Rachel often arrive to school late. This is the sixth school for Mackenzie, a third grader, and the second school for kindergartner Rachel. It turns out that they are getting themselves to school every day and often arrive dirty, hungry, and with messy hair. According to the girls, mom sleeps a lot, and there is no dad in the picture. They each have a different dad. After many conversations about school, nothing changes. Mom takes them out of school for more than a week with no phone call. When previous schools are contacted, it sounds like this is the way it has always been. With this information, a home visit follows. The condition of the apartment is appalling. Even more disturbing than the chaos that is taking place is that the five-year-old answers the door with a dead boa constrictor around her neck. It died while they were gone for a week. Ultimately little Rachel ends up with a horrible case of infatigo, which is only treated when the school insists that she receive medical attention. A community volunteer has to drive the family to the doctor because the mom's car was impounded due to a DUI. Things seem to be spiraling out of control. With no changes, and after many efforts to support the family, Child Protective Services is contacted. The school gives the girls an alarm clock and incentives to get to school on time. They feed them breakfast when they arrive. They begin to attend school every day and begin to make some progress. The school takes a different approach. They support them, love them, and provide a safe, consistent environment every day, and the girls begin to flourish. Much like Precious in the movie of the same name, the reality is that the school won't be able to change this mom. The only hope for these girls is to instill in them the importance and value of learning and help them become motivated to achieve school success on their own.

The key to supporting Tier Four parents is supporting their children. The key to supporting their children is found in the way that we unify our approach as staff members. Chapter Eleven will offer details on how schools can do just that. As you read, keep the Tier Four children in mind. Remain cognizant of their heartbreak, of their challenging existence. Let that understanding drive you, not to enable their negative behaviors, but rather to find a new and better approach to connect with them.

Now that we have examined each tier in detail, take the time to try and evaluate your parents again. Using the Differentiated Parenting Support model, where do you think your parents are in the four tiers? What percentage of your parents are Tier One? Tier Two? Tier Three? Tier Four? For the Tier Three and Tier Four parents, how many of them are struggling to survive? One of the common factors we have correlated to some of the Tier Two, Tier Three, and Tier Four parents is that they are missing basic needs. Helping parents with their basic needs should never be looked at as a handout. The idea is never to take on their responsibilities. Rather, it is to take advantage of the opportunities that exist when parents need our help and utilize those opportunities for building stronger relationships with them. Remember, if we can help families meet their basic needs, then perhaps parents can shift their focus from survival to their children's education.

Theory to Practice

 How many Tier Four families do you have?

 In what ways can you support the students of Tier Four parents?

Key Concepts

1
Community Outreach

2
Community Collaborative Partnerships

3
Community Outreach Activities

10

Community
Outreach

*"If you are not part of the solution, you are part of the problem.
The price of greatness is responsibility"*

~ Winston Churchill

I had been around police before, but never in a room with so many
of them in my life. I was overwhelmed when I walked into the school
library to a sea of navy blue. There were more than a dozen policemen
from the San Diego Police Department and another dozen community
members. That all of these policemen and other community members
made the time to come to a meeting to support Los Pen left me almost
speechless. Which was a problem, because I was scheduled to make

a presentation to them about a grant opportunity for our school and community. Once I caught my breath, this is what I shared:

Six weeks earlier, the principal and I had made a decision to attempt to apply for a $300,000 school policing grant from the state of California. Our hope was to secure this grant funding so that we could provide more student and family services at school and also to increase the presence of the police in the neighborhood to try to decrease crime. After gathering school and community data, I met with a representative of the police department as well as individual community members to determine how to share our plans. In addition to data, I was also seeking their support for the grant because one of the grant requirements was to collaborate with the local police and community members. The meeting was an opportunity to share the data and to outline the proposed plans for the grant. With everyone's support, we wrote the grant and fortunately received the funding to implement our strategies.

The lessons learned from this experience were abundant, but few of them were related to money. One of the most valuable lessons was the power of community collaborative partnerships. The collaborative partnerships were so strong and powerful that at the end of the grant period, all of the collaborative members requested to continue our monthly meetings. Seven years later, we continue to collaborate monthly about how to enhance the school and the community.

Community Collaborative Partnerships

Community partnerships can be an integral piece to successfully supporting families. With strong community partners, all of the outreach activities can be managed by volunteers and require very little work on the part of school personnel. Primarily, school personnel needs to gather and disseminate information. This can be the task of just one staff member. That person serves as the school coordinator for community outreach activities. Teachers, counselors, principals, health techs, school secretaries, or any other willing staff member can fill the community outreach school coordinator role.

Although partnerships take time to establish initially, once established they require very little effort and reap tremendous rewards. Community outreach can start small and grow. Begin with one activity and then add others bit by bit. With strong community partners, the partners often initiate, organize, and implement activities. And here's the great thing—it doesn't cost any money! So how can you form these community partnerships? Here are four simple steps:

1. Identify community members

2. Contact members by phone, mail, or in person

3. Establish a collaborative group

4. Meet monthly to discuss the school and community

Possible members may include churches, businesses, PTA, police, fire, city councils, service organizations, YMCA, and members of your school district. One way to identify and recruit members is to attend local community meetings and share information about your school.

Community Partnership Brainstorm

1. *Who are your community partners?*

Research the agencies and organizations near your school. Connect with members of these agencies and organizations to facilitate a relationship.

2. *Who can be your school contact?*

Think about staff members who may be interested and have the time to be the primary contact for community partners.

3. *Which of your families need support?*

Get to know your families. Gather information from students, parents, and teachers. Create and maintain a confidential database.

4. *What are your agency resources?*

Do some research to find out what resources are available. Talk to county agencies, local service clubs, and other schools.

5. *What will be your first step?*

Take action! Do something! Come up with a plan! Momentum is as powerful as any money.

Right now, take the time to brainstorm about the potential for community partnerships.

Community Outreach

Once our partnerships were established, we began to work on community outreach. Community outreach evolved out of the recognition that many of our inactive parents are struggling to have the basic needs of the family met. As we set out to further understand our parents in the four tiers, Maslow's triangle was a helpful reference. Abraham Maslow was a professor of psychology at Brandeis University and founded humanistic psychology. He created a visual aid, which he called the Hierarchy of Needs, to represent the levels of human needs, psychological and physical. Maslow's theory was included in his 1954 book *Motivation and Personality*. According to Maslow's theory, to reach the level of self-actualization, people must not only reach each level of need first, but also master each of the prior needs of physiology, safety, love, and esteem.

MASLOW'S HIERARCHY OF NEEDS TRIANGLE

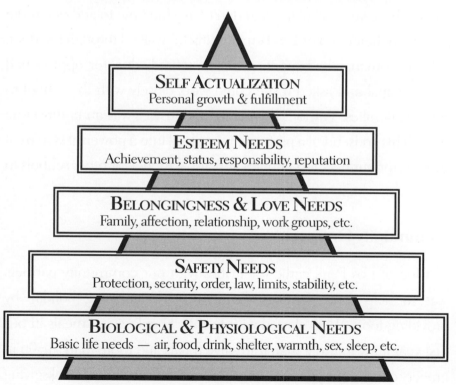

SELF ACTUALIZATION
Personal growth & fulfillment

ESTEEM NEEDS
Achievement, status, responsibility, reputation

BELONGINGNESS & LOVE NEEDS
Family, affection, relationship, work groups, etc.

SAFETY NEEDS
Protection, security, order, law, limits, stability, etc.

BIOLOGICAL & PHYSIOLOGICAL NEEDS
Basic life needs — air, food, drink, shelter, warmth, sex, sleep, etc.

In an effort to better understand our parents, we began to relate our Tier One, Tier Two, Tier Three, and Tier Four parents to the levels of the triangle. We knew that many of our Tier Three and Tier Four families were at the bottom of Maslow's triangle and struggling to get their basic needs met. Take a look at Maslow's triangle. Maslow believes that every human wants to reach self-actualization. Using this as a perspective, where do you think your parents fit in Maslow's triangle?

When families are at the bottom of Maslow's Hierarchy of Needs, they are in "survival mode." School is low on the list of priorities. To help children arrive at school, ready to learn, basic needs must be met. How can schools do that? Most schools don't have a system or method in place to support a family's basic needs. Additionally, most educators already have very full plates and don't have the time to add one more project to their day. For Los Pen, a "miracle" walked through the door. A local woman, who happened to be a retired educator, approached the principal and asked if she could work closely with the school to support families. Without hesitation, the answer was an enthusiastic "yes." This godsend of a partnership evolved into a powerful system of support for our neediest families and also a model for other schools to follow.

Community Outreach

One of Los Pen's earliest activities with our community partners was to help some families during the Thanksgiving holiday by providing food. What started with twenty Thanksgiving meals in our first year grew to more than thirty-five meals and more than $1,300 in grocery cards in the years to come. So successful was our Thanksgiving endeavor that we decided to offer similar support during Christmas. Becky, Los Pen's volunteer community partner liaison, created and implemented a program called "Adopt-a-Family." Adopt-a-Family's purpose is to provide some holiday spirit and to fulfill some wishes for families in poverty. Identified families are invited to complete a wish list. This list is then provided to community members who work to fulfill their wishes. Right before the holidays, volunteers deliver the wish list items to participating families. This is something that started small and grew, or should I say exploded! In the first year, twenty families were adopted. Twenty became forty, forty became eighty, and today there are well more than one hundred families adopted on a yearly basis. After seven years of outreach, both of these programs have grown to support and help some of our neediest families at Los Pen while also serving as a model to other schools and community organizations. The Adopt-a-Family model has been embraced by dozens of schools across the country.

The impact that such outreach makes on a family is often difficult to articulate, but is touchingly captured in an email from one of the mothers affected by this community support. While the names have been changed to protect the privacy of this family, the letter has been left in its original form with no corrections for spelling or grammar.

"Hi I'm (Susie's) mom and froom the Family we would like to say thankyou from every inch of our hearts to you and others who helped you help our family. if you only knew what these holidays are going to be like for us with so much happening to us so quick and back to back and

me being a single parent taking care of mines and my sisters kids it is really hard but you guys are so great i have never been so filled with hope and great faith to be able to give them more then just I'm sorry but idont have it and I'm sorry i cant do this or that it hurts youknow and you guys took so much heartache away from me this year and i'amtrullytrully thankful and i know they will be to. Thankyou for helping me keep my faith and believing and not letting it get me depressed and much more. God Bless with lots of LOVE from our Family. Happy Happy Holidays...."

You see, it's not just about giving away material things. It's also about providing hope and encouragement to a mother on the brink of depression. It's about children experiencing and regaining faith in their mom or dad, as they have somehow provided the special Christmas morning that has been missing for years. It's about caring, character, and love that exemplifies the word "community." And while it is terrific for those who receive, it is far more enjoyable to those involved in the giving.

If your school has been reluctant to reach out to your neediest families, give it another try. Benefit from our experiences and use some of the strategies that we have found to be effective. The system for this Adopt-a-Family endeavor has been refined over the years, but there are primarily six simple steps.

Adopt-a-Family — Six Simple Steps

1. Identify families from teachers or the families themselves.

2. Gather information about families using the Holiday Information Sheet.

3. Number each Information Sheet as it is returned to facilitate confidentiality. Families can then be identified by numbers, to keep their names confidential.

4. Create a database at the school for tracking purposes.

5. Provide information to community partners.

6. Community partners do the rest. They find donors and volunteers to make deliveries to the homes of the families.

The Adopt-a-Family process begins in October. Following is a sample of the Holiday Information Sheet that is sent home to families to complete and return to school.

Community Outreach Activities

Community outreach activities can also extend throughout the year. These activities are managed by community volunteers, which reduces the impact on school personnel. Year-round support can include food, clothing, school supplies, household items, furniture, rides to appointments, assistance completing forms, or help connecting with community resources such as healthcare. Some examples of year-round support that can be provided are mentioned here.

═══ HOLIDAY INFORMATION SHEET ═══

Several community organizations have offered to sponsor families for the holiday season. Please complete the form below for every member in your household, including adults. All information remains confidential and is used by the organization to purchase gifts for your family.

Family Name: _____

First Name	School	Age	Sex	Clothing sizes	Shoe size	Wish List
				Top: Pants:		
				Top: Pants:		
				Top: Pants:		
				Top: Pants:		

The information below will be kept separate from your list and will be used only to contact you for delivery.

Name: _____

Address: _____

Daytime Phone #: _____

Student Name: _____

Classroom: _____

Year-Round Support

Weekly Bread: Most bakeries bake fresh bread daily. Anything that is left at the end of the day will not be used in the bakery the next day. Rather than throwing all of the delicious items out, local volunteers can pick up the bread and other items at closing time. To facilitate easy distribution, volunteers divide the donations into family-sized portions using donated fruit and vegetable bags from a local grocery store. These volunteers can deliver the donated items to school the next morning before school starts. At Los Pen, about twenty-five parents stop by the school every Wednesday to pick up bread and other bakery items donated by Panera. Contact your local bakery and arrange a face-to-face meeting with the owner, expressing your appreciation in advance for any support that they can offer. What may start as a few loaves of bread could easily turn into bags of items that support dozens of families.

Monthly Groceries: With a little work on the part of community volunteers, families can receive free groceries each month. Food distributors often find that they need to dispose of food items when they get close to expiration dates rather than deliver them to stores. With a coordinated effort, rather than allowing the food items to go in the trash, volunteers can pick up the food and provide it to families. Research the community food banks. Check with some local churches, as they may already have a relationship with a food bank. Or contact your local county agencies to find resources.

Summer Programs: Have you ever noticed that many of your students show up on the first day of school with major fluctuations in their weight? We did, and found out that it was due to a lack of consistent nourishment throughout the summer. These same students turned out to be the children who received free breakfast and lunch during the school year. When the summer came, their guaranteed two meals a day often turned into a bag of chips and soda three times a day. Because of this, local church members invite children to the church for hot lunches and fun activities twice every week during the summer. At the end of the summer, the volunteers provide backpacks and school supplies for all of the students who participated. As you can imagine, this is an enormous help to the families taking part. Such an effort would have never been achieved without our terrific partnership with the faith-based community. Determine which churches are near your school and contact them to establish a relationship. Or speak to staff members who are actively involved with a church to see if there may be interest in working with some families during the summer.

Faith-Based Organizations: Most churches actively seek ways to support their communities and local families. They have tremendous resources and people who are anxious and willing to volunteer to help families. So don't shy away from faith-based organizations. Sometimes schools are hesitant to work with churches because of the guideline to "separate church and state." Churches can provide some of the most incredible support to needy families. At Los Pen, for more than ten years, New Hope Church has sponsored a before- and afterschool program on the school campus, for more than one hundred of our poorest families. They call the program BLAST: Building Leaders as Students Today. These students arrive on campus as early as 6:30 a.m. and stay until 6 p.m. When the program first started, it was completely

126

free, funded by an afterschool grant from the City of San Diego. Once the grant was no longer available, parents needed to contribute. The current cost is $75.00 per month, but 30 percent of our neediest families receive full scholarships to participate. This has been a tremendous support to many of our families. It provides a safe place for children while their parents are working. In all of the years, months, weeks, and days we have had this partnership with New Hope, the church never has violated the separation of church and state. It offers a safe haven for children with a heart focused not on religious beliefs, but more so on a desire to serve humanity.

This successful relationship with New Hope inspired additional strong connections with other local churches. For example, a women's group from a church gathered luxury items, such as lotions and creams, for Mother's Day, put them in beautiful gift bags and delivered them to school. When mothers came to pick up their weekly delivery of free bread, they each received a wonderful Mother's Day gift! Another church, PQ Lutheran, provides lunches in the summer and delivers bread every week. Church members also provided more than one hundred coats to children in the fall. Take an inventory of the churches that may be interested in establishing a relationship with your school and supporting your families.

Qualifying for Support

How do schools qualify families to receive support? On our campus, as at most schools that have created a community support system, we don't. If a school attempts to create an application or minimum income requirement in order to offer support, the process may become quite cumbersome and complicated. In fact, it can be a roadblock to action, as all of your focus is placed on the bureaucracy of the system. Therefore, a great guideline is this: If a family appears to need some support, offer it—with no strings attached. It's that easy. Does this create an opportunity for some people who may take advantage of the situation and ask or accept help when they truly don't need it? Sure. But in the seven years that Los Pen has been working to support families through community outreach, with the hundreds of families that we have offered support to, we have only been taken advantage of on one occasion. With a track record like that, I'd say that trusting your parents is worth the risk, wouldn't you?

To determine which families need support, gather information and maintain a database. Information can be gathered from students, parents, or teachers. When new families arrive at school, teachers can complete an information sheet like the one seen here.

Once information has been gathered, it can be passed on to the community partners. This information is then used to support families during the holidays or throughout the year. Here are some simple guidelines for community outreach. The information is gathered with parent permission to ensure confidentiality.

COMMUNITY OUTREACH FAMILY INFORMATION

Teacher Name: _____

Please list any students whom you perceive need extra support. Mark the appropriate column to indicate which support might benefit this family the most.

Student Name	Immediate Needs	Weekly Bread	Monthly Food	Thanksgiving	Holiday Wish List

Immediate Needs: Clothing and household items for families in need

Weekly Bread: Bread delivered to school

Monthly Food: Identified families receive food and dairy products.

Thanksgiving: Meals and gift cards

Holiday Adopt-a-Family: Community groups adopt families and provide some holiday wishes.

HOLIDAY SUPPORT

1. Identify families from teachers or the families themselves.

2. Gather information about families using the Holiday Information Sheet.

3. Number each Information Sheet as it is returned to facilitate confidentiality.

4. Create a database at the school for tracking purposes.

5. Provide information to community partners.

6. Community partners do the rest. They find donors and volunteers to make deliveries to the homes of the families.

YEAR-ROUND SUPPORT

1. Gather information about families by connecting with teachers and/or the families themselves.

2. Contact families to determine what their needs are and if they are receptive to receiving support.

3. Ask if you may give their name and number to your community partner.

4. Email or phone your community partner.

5. Let it happen!

Theory to Practice

 Brainstorm some potential community outreach partners.

 Establish a community collaborative monthly meeting.

 Create a list of possible community outreach activities.

Key Concepts

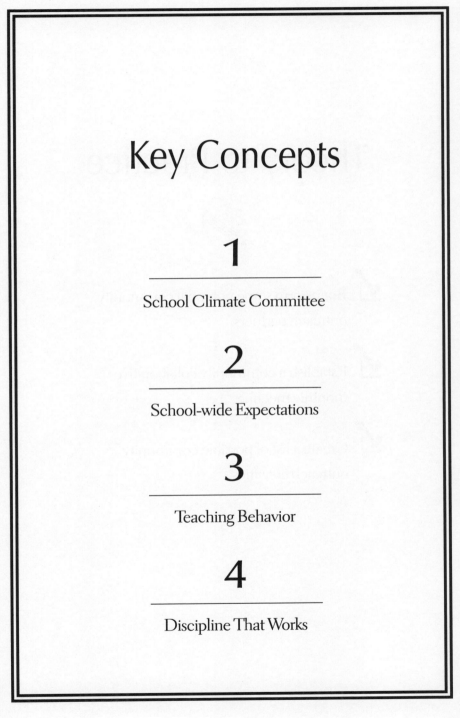

1

School Climate Committee

2

School-wide Expectations

3

Teaching Behavior

4

Discipline That Works

11

Home to School Connection

"Coming together is a beginning.
Keeping together is progress.
Working together is success."

~ Henry Ford

Educators across America know that academic success is increased when children are socially and emotionally prepared. Creating and implementing a climate with clear behavior expectations not only supports student success, it supports parent success. With an effective school climate, students become "ready to learn." A positive school climate supports parents in their role of helping their children become ready to learn by serving as a model for strategies that can transfer into their own expectations of behavior at home.

133

There are many examples of the adversity and challenges that children and families must deal with every day. I am sure you can name dozens of children you work with who come from very difficult situations. At Los Pen, more than half of the students are from broken homes. Forty percent of the apartments across the street from our school are populated by single moms with an average income of less than $14,000 a year. In almost every classroom at Los Pen, there are students who have a parent in jail or prison. Several children live with parents who have mental health or substance abuse issues. There are children living with grandparents, relatives, or foster parents. In spite of these hardships, all of these children deserve the opportunity to be educated in a way that prepares them for college and offers them hope to shift the cycle of poverty. This is a tremendous responsibility for our schools today. It becomes more challenging with some of the adversity that these children and families experience. Imagine how you would feel as a child if this story were about you:

> There are three children in the family and they are all about eighteen months apart. Dad works all day and evening, leaving mom at home with the children. Unfortunately for the children, Mom has substance abuse issues and ignores the children all day, leaving them completely unsupervised. The oldest child assumes responsibility for the younger ones, trying to feed them, change their diapers, and keep them safe. Whenever Mom goes out, she locks the two oldest children in the hall closet to play with Legos until she returns hours later, often forcing them to urinate in the closet.

> When the oldest child is five, one evening mom takes the dog for

a walk and never comes back. She is hit by a car and permanently brain-damaged. She has to spend the rest of her life in a wheelchair and a special facility. Her children never see her again. In some ways, the children may be better off without her, except that their father remains disconnected and emotionally uninvolved with the children. He continues to work long hours and relegates the raising of his children to their grandmother.

Kids like these arrive at school, and we focus on promoting academic success for them. We want them to follow the school rules, even though they've had no consistency in rules at home or been part of a school that "taught" them the rules of the school. Do you think appropriate behavior comes naturally to kids like these? Do you think following rules are on their list of priorities? Are they ready to learn? This is only one story, from one school. The question is not, "Who has harder kids to work with?" The fact is that you too could match stories like these tenfold. The real question is, "What are we doing for these children that has not already been done?"

Children arrive at our schools with many different issues. These issues often translate into misbehavior, which often gets in the way of learning. Unfortunately, this misbehavior doesn't just keep the misbehaving students from learning—their disruptions affect the learning opportunity of their classmates. We need to manage and modify this misbehavior. It is imperative that we proactively create a climate that will support all students learning.

When I arrived at Los Pen in 2003 as the new school counselor, misbehavior and discipline issues were of great concern. One of my first priorities was to increase social skills and emotional health while decreasing the number of discipline referrals. I knew that I would not be able to accomplish this on my own, so I worked collaboratively with a team to accomplish positive changes in student behavior and discipline. As much success as Los Pen was experiencing with academics, I knew that we could enhance this academic success by creating stronger social and emotional support for our students. With that in mind, we created an exceptional system around the concept of unifying our message with our school climate. Today, this system supports children and families and also models effective strategies for parents to work on with their children.

School Climate Committee

Initially, I collaborated with the principal and our student services teacher, who works in a capacity much like an assistant principal. The three of us met every single week. We talked about students, teachers, and parents. We discussed the most high-risk students with the highest number of referrals and began to develop strategies to support them. As we worked, we knew that we not only needed to support individual students and families, but we also needed to create a comprehensive school-wide system that would support all students. We began to assess needs in the areas of behavior, discipline, and school climate. We examined data, talked to staff, students, and parents, and set goals and priorities. We reviewed discipline data to create a list of major concerns and pinpoint where on campus negative behavior was taking place. In addition, we used discipline data to determine which staff members had the highest number of discipline incidents.

What we found, and what you likely will find as well, is that 80 percent of the discipline referrals came from 20 percent of the teachers. Information like this was invaluable. Simply by looking at numbers, we were able to pinpoint the staff members, both certificated and classified, who needed more strategies as they worked with students. In addition, we were able to capitalize on the staff members who did a spectacular job of working with negative behaviors and utilize them as a resource. We asked them a number of questions: What were they doing differently? Were they just lucky to get some of the most manageable children or was the students' good behavior because of the way they work with them? What is the climate in their classrooms? How do they establish expectations and routines? How do they teach what the behavior expectations look like and sound like? How do they enforce the behavior expectations when rules are broken? Make the time to visit these classrooms and observe the strategies that the teachers are using with their students. Talk to the teachers and the kids.

After our exploration, we found that the teachers with the greatest success had the following things in common:

- Their behavior management system was clear and concise.
- They set expectations that were lofty and held students to them.
- They consistently reinforced appropriate behavior and modeled character as the leader of the classroom.
- They provided daily instruction on how to achieve academic and social success.

In hindsight, none of this was surprising. What was surprising, however, is how easy these teachers made it look. What's more, all of the teachers viewed their instruction as second nature because they had developed positive habits that stayed with them throughout the course of their career. Our directive was clear. We needed to spotlight teachers with these habits and participate in activities that began to develop similar habits school-wide. Rather than hold solely students accountable for their mistakes, we would need to employ methods to be proactive in teaching acceptable behavior to our students. This method of "teaching behavior" became the focal point for our school climate system. How did it work? Well, the data speaks for itself.

In our *first year* of making changes by implementing an effective school climate system, Los Pen's discipline decreased by 48 percent. Discipline referrals went from 233 in a year to 121. What does it mean to cut your discipline referrals in half? If you consider that discipline referrals, on average, remove a student from the classroom for at least a half an hour, for 233 referrals that is a loss of 116 hours of learning! What a waste of time and resources. And because any loss of time in class for at-risk students is crucial, this decrease of referrals was significant. When discipline incidents go down, appropriate behavior goes up. There is an increase in respect for one another and loyalty to the school as a community. Not to mention the effect on the climate when there are fewer discipline incidents taking place on the playground, in the hallways, or throughout the classrooms — the school becomes a much more pleasant place to spend your day.

This system didn't work just at Los Pen. As other schools learned about the system that Los Pen created, they implemented similar systems and experienced positive results. In fact, in 2006, the Poway Unified School District Student Services department applied for a federal counseling grant. The grant was modeled after many of the approaches Los Pen had put into place with the culture, exceptional systems, and college readiness. All six of the other Title I schools in the district utilized the Los Pen School Climate System. The results were dramatic. During the three-year grant period, all of our schools experienced a significant decrease in discipline referrals and an increase in social skills, resulting in increased academic success. This exceptional school climate system works.

If you are committed to creating an exceptional school climate system, I suggest you start by creating a school climate committee. Recruit a teacher from every grade level who is willing to work to create a comprehensive system. History shows that effective collaboration of a committee of stakeholders enhances the effectiveness and success of any challenging undertaking. The other benefit of collaboration is that it translates into stronger ownership of the system that is created, which ultimately enhances the successful implementation and sustainability.

Across the country, schools that have implemented school climate systems modeled after Los Pen's have also realized very positive results. These schools have learned about this effective system from TurnAround Schools, the company Damen Lopez cofounded in 2006. Damen and TurnAround Schools associates work with schools, districts, and educational organizations throughout the country in an effort to support the development of six exceptional systems, resulting in academic success for all. For more information about these exceptional systems, read Damen's book *No Excuses University*. As a TurnAround Schools associate, I have been able to share our exceptional school climate system with thousands of educators. Many of these educators have taken the lessons learned from TurnAround and realized increased academic success for their students. As you go forward in creating your own school climate system, refer to the following steps:

1) Establish clear expectations.

2) Teach behavior to help students meet your expectations.

3) Reinforce expectations daily.

4) Correct negative behavior with an effective discipline system.

(Remember: Student, staff, and parent expectations are established with the Code of Conduct covered in Chapter Six.)

SCHOOL-WIDE EXPECTATIONS

A Code of Conduct (Chapter Six) acts as your school's list of expectations. Once the expectations are established, behaviors need to be taught. We cannot assume that students understand what the Code of Conduct looks like in every situation; therefore, we teach. Teaching expectations within the Code of Conduct is a very effective way to prevent misbehavior. Rather than allowing teachers to individually decide the expectations for specific behaviors, staffs need to collaborate and agree on universal school-wide behavior. This is particularly critical when it comes to the geographical areas of the school that are shared. Expectations should be clearly defined in areas on campus such as the office, cafeteria, playground, bathrooms, hallways, library, and computer lab. The same holds true for other shared activities that occur daily like line behavior, coming to school on time, and turning in homework.

Explicit Examples of What Behavior Looks Like

Kyrene de los Niños is an elementary school in Tempe, Arizona. Serving a population made up largely of second-language Hispanic students, Niños offers a school climate that has enhanced the social success of its very needy students. The fiftieth school to join the NEU Network of Schools, Niños adopted the Los Pen's School Climate System and then took it a step further. The staff not only created a climate that capitalized on a proactive approach to teaching behavior, but also developed a comprehensive form with descriptions of what each behavior looks like and doesn't look like. Such a step supports consistency that is appreciated by parents and deserved by students. A sample of this chart is shown in the appendix and can also be found on the CD that came with this book.

NEU Prep

As I mentioned earlier, students often arrive with a different set of rules and behavior. What they are allowed to do at home may not align with what we will allow them to do at school. Thus we must purposefully and deliberately teach behavior expectations. A systematic approach to teaching behaviors is what we refer to as NEU Prep. NEU Prep is a format that is used by each teacher as they take their students through a morning meeting every day. This daily meeting lasts about fifteen minutes. The purpose of NEU Prep is to enrich the climate and tone of learning through merging social and intellectual learning. The focus is:

- Getting students ready for the school day
- Preparing them to learn academics
- Teaching home versus school rules
- Teaching academic language
- Explicitly teaching routines and procedures
- Gaining skills necessary for college and life success

Everyone, including the teacher, sits in a circle on the floor or in chairs so that all participants can see each other. The structure of NEU Prep is divided into three parts: greeting, sharing, and activity.

Greeting: The greeting sets a positive tone, helps to provide a sense of belonging, and develops a sense of community and respect among students. There are many different activities for greeting. Students may simply say to the student next to them in the circle, "Good morning, Ke'Andre." Then Ke'Andre responds, "Good morning, Salma." Ke'Andre then turns to the student on the other side of him and says, "Good morning, Ernesto." And Ernesto responds with, "Good morning Ke'Andre" and then turns to the student next to him. This continues all the way around the circle until every student has greeted someone by name.

Sharing: This part of NEU Prep is used primarily to teach behavior or academic expectations. In the first twenty days of school, every teacher in the entire school is addressing the exact same behavior. After that, grade level teams choose topics. Teams meet every Wednesday for professional collaboration. Based on the needs

THE FIRST 20 DAYS

Day 1	Campus safety
Day 2	Walking/waiting in lines
Day 3	Playground rules
Day 4	After school and dismissal behavior
Day 5	Assembly behavior
Day 6	Academic expectations
Day 7	End of the day packing-up
Day 8	Cafeteria etiquette
Day 9	Hallway behavior/hall passes
Day 10	Transitions to/from classrooms
Day 11	Bathroom etiquette/procedure
Day 12	Guest entering/phone procedure
Day 13	Interacting with peers
Day 14	Talking with adults
Day 15	Voice level on campus/in class
Day 16	Character Counts!
Day 17	Classroom materials
Day 18	Review classroom management
Day 19	Guest teacher behavior
Day 20	Rainy day behavior

of the students in the grade level, teachers generate the topics that will be addressed during the sharing time of NEU Prep.

Activity: If there is time, the class participates in a brief math or other academic activity. This contributes to the culture of the classroom community by allowing students to see each other's strengths. Taking turns, cooperation, and problem-solving can be modeled.

NEU Prep is an excellent way to build community and to reinforce school-wide expectations. It sets the tone for the day and helps students get ready to learn. It creates clarity in the school climate, utilizing the common language of the Code of Conduct, and provides consistency of school-wide behavior expectations. This leads to students not only being more successful with their social behaviors; it translates into academic success.

Universal Classroom Management Plan

As part of our school climate system, our staff agreed that to create consistency, each and every classroom needed to have a similar behavior management plan. With every teacher using the same plan, students know exactly what the expectations are and what happens if they choose not to follow the expected Code of Conduct. No matter what classroom they are in or what grade they are in, the rules and consequences are the same. This strongly supports smooth transitions from one grade level to the next. It eliminates the gray areas and the confusion. Behavior expectations are clear and consistent. The school climate committee worked together to come up with a Universal Classroom Management Plan. Here is a sample of the plan for second through fifth grade. In the appendix, you can find the sample for kindergarten and first grade.

CLASSROOM MANAGEMENT PLAN
(GRADES 2-5)

*"Character is doing the right thing,
even when no one is watching"*

CODE OF CONDUCT:

I will be trustworthy.   I will be respectful.   I will be fair.
I will be responsible.   I will be a good citizen.   I will be caring.

If you choose to break the code of conduct (consequences):

1ST TIME: **CAUTION: YELLOW**
Sign in the book.

2ND TIME: **STOP: RED**
Sign in the book. Fill out the rethinking paper

3RD TIME: **TIME-OUT:**
Sign in the Book
Take a Break in another class
Fill out the time-out letter/home to parent
Possible Loss of Recess

4TH TIME OR SEVERE DISRUPTION:
Immediately sent to the office
Fill out character violation

POSITIVE REINFORCEMENT:
Praise — Daily
Positive Notes Home — Random
Character Counts Award
Individual Classroom Reinforcement

We have read and discussed this classroom management plan and
will support and honor the plan throughout the year.

_____   _____

Parent Signature   Student Signature

RETHINKING LETTER

You are receiving a second warning about your negative choices. Please think about what you have done and answer these questions.

1. What did I do to receive my yellow warning?

   _____

   _____

2. What did I do to receive my red warning?

   _____

   _____

3. How did your choice affect others?

   _____

   _____

4. What caused your negative choice?

   _____

   _____

5. What could you do better next time?

   _____

   _____

Please check one:

_____ I get the point. I will try harder in class.

_____ I don't understand. We need to talk about my behavior.

_____   _____
Parent Signature   Student Signature

Handbooks

Once you have established a code of conduct based on a common language of character traits, capture the information in handbooks. Create handbooks for staff, students, and parents. These handbooks provide guidelines and specific information to reinforce clarity in climate based on your common language. A list of the topics included in the Student Handbook, Staff Handbook (Endorsement), and Parent Handbook can be found in the appendix. A sample of the student handbook is also in the appendix. Samples of the Student Handbook, Parent Handbook, and Staff Handbook (Endorsement) are on the CD that came with this book.

Creating handbooks was fairly simple because we already had much of the information in some form or another. For our Student Handbook, we took our outdated School Rulebook and changed the contents to align with our Code of Conduct. We kept a similar format design, but we no longer felt that we needed to have a list of thirty or forty rules. Many rules are already included in the district discipline document that all students and parents are required to sign in the beginning of the year. This document covers each and every discipline and behavior expectation of our school district, specifically addressing weapons, drugs, academic honesty, harassment, and violence. Having the district discipline paperwork allows us to make our school rules in our handbook much simpler. As I mentioned, we have only six school rules, the six character traits of Character Counts that we developed into our Code of Conduct.

To develop the staff handbook, which eventually evolved into our current NEU Endorsement, we simply gathered all of the critical information and guidelines for staff that were already being utilized and put them together in one place. The NEU Endorsement became our playbook. It includes our school goal and all of the exceptional systems. It also includes the Staff Code of Conduct, expectations to provide college readiness, and our yearly master calendar. The calendar is very extensive, including dates for report cards, assessments, articulations, conferences, and parent meetings. Additionally, the handbook includes the system for discipline and the system that our yard duties have been trained to use for discipline and behavior concerns.

For the Parent Handbook, we gathered all the information that we normally provide to parents and then brainstormed what additional information might be helpful to our parents. With very little effort, we were able to create a comprehensive, user-friendly handbook. It includes the Code of Conduct for the school as well as a more specific Parent Code of Conduct. For example, in the area of responsibility, we included "Review papers from school and return them in a timely manner." Under trustworthiness we listed "Pick your child up from school on time." In the area of caring we included "Tell your children that you love them." And one of my personal favorites is in citizenship: "Obey all traffic laws, especially the ones in the school parking lot." As you can see from the list above, we include several items about the campus, some helpful parent information, and information about college readiness. Samples of all of the handbooks are included in the appendix.

Visual Reminders

Visual reminders are powerful. Permeate the campus with the

common language. If character traits become the school rules and Code of Conduct, utilize the character traits throughout the school. Create an 11-by-17 in. poster with the Code of Conduct for all students to sign, pledging that they will follow the code. Change the discipline referrals and school rewards, and develop classroom management plans based on the Code of Conduct. Weave the Code of Conduct into classroom lessons. Continue to refer to the Code of Conduct and the character traits throughout the year at school assemblies. Choose one character trait a month to focus on. Teach students about character and the Code of Conduct in the classroom, at assemblies, and with announcements over the school's public address system. Instead of using random student planners, find some student planners that relate to character.

Place posters about character in every classroom, the library, the computer lab, the office, and throughout the entire school. Consider creating murals about the character traits in outdoor areas near the playground. Always include information about character traits on the school marquee and school newsletter. Find every opportunity to talk about and relate everything back to the character traits and the Code of Conduct.

This Code of Conduct based on character ultimately becomes part of the school culture. It becomes part of all of the stakeholders. When you start hearing students referring to the traits and Code of Conduct, you know that you have been successful in infusing the school culture with this common language. At Los Pen, every year students running for Student Council offices give speeches to the student body. In recent years, I was so excited to hear these students referring to the character traits and the Code of Conduct. During their speeches, they assert that they are students of character and always abide by the Code of Conduct. They speak of character very naturally, because it has become part of their daily language and conversations.

Setting and teaching behavior expectations works for the majority of students to help them learn and practice behavior that supports academic success, but, of course, not for all. Even with the best Code of Conduct and school climate system in place, children will still misbehave. Why?

Understanding Misbehavior

All children want to belong and to be successful. This is a very basic human drive. Often, however, their poor behavior gets in the way of success. Why do some children misbehave? Are they born that way? Do they come into the world with an evil spirit? Experts will tell you that children misbehave because they are discouraged. The challenge is figuring out what is causing their discouragement. Many times, we don't have to look very far. As we get to know some of these children, we may discover that they have very challenging home lives. Other times, after a short time in a classroom, it becomes evident that they are struggling academically. Whatever the cause, children, particularly elementary age children, are not very articulate about expressing their feelings of discouragement. Instead, they misbehave as a form of communication.

This misbehavior is often exhibited in the form of attention-seeking actions. They are desperate for attention, any attention, and they will do whatever they can to get it. Discouraged children will play the class clown, constantly ask for help, talk without raising their hand, engage in a power struggle, or act out in defiance. Understanding their behavior can help teachers take proactive actions to prevent the unwanted behavior. For children seeking attention, provide positive attention whenever possible. For children looking for some power or control, offer choices. When prevention of misbehavior doesn't work, it is necessary to provide consequences so that children can learn how to change their behavior.

A Time For Discipline

What happens for students at your school when they are sent to the office for behavior issues? This is another area of our school climate system that we changed at Los Pen. Think about your school's discipline plan, and ask, "Are we trying to change student behavior or are we trying to make them pay for it?" This is an important question to ask. If we are trying to change behavior, we are talking about discipline. If we are trying to make students pay for their behavior, then we are talking about punishment. There is a big difference in punishment versus discipline.

Discipline comes from the word "disciple." To disciple means "to teach." If we are practicing discipline, our system is about teaching. The problem with punishment is that it rarely works. Punishment may often create passive-aggressive behavior. There is a cute saying about passive-aggressive behavior: "It's like a puppy—while he is licking your face, he may be peeing on your lap." Punishment is about external control. As long as the authority figure or disciplinarian is present, the child is likely to behave, due to fear. When the threat of punishment is not imminent because the authority figure is not present, many children will choose to do whatever they want, whether it is right or wrong. Discipline, on the other hand, tends to develop more intrinsic control. Discipline comes from learning from experiences and consequences. For most people, when their experiences with their choices result in negative consequences, they will choose to change their choices of behavior to get a more positive outcome. So how can we help children learn this lesson? How can we help them process an experience and learn to make a different choice in the future?

At school, one of the simpler strategies to put into place is to change students' experiences when they are sent to the office. Rather than adults doing all of the thinking and talking, have the students do the work. In most schools, when students are sent to the office, they meet with an administrator. They discuss the behavior, and the adult tells the children that they broke a rule and what to do next time to avoid getting into trouble. The problem with this is that all children hear is, "Blah, blah, blah, blah." The directions may frequently just go right into one ear and out of the other.

At Los Pen, when students are sent to the office because of discipline issues, they are greeted with three questions. Depending on the age of the students, either the questions are asked by the counselor or principal, or students may receive the questions on a clipboard and be expected to provide a written response. The questions are:

1. What happened?

2. What caused that to happen?

3. What can you do differently in the future?

Now here's where it can sometimes get a little tricky. Is it possible that a student could respond to question number three with, "I don't know"?

152

Of course it is possible. Why do children say "I don't know" so much? Because they know about the Fifth Amendment, that whatever you say can and will be used against you in a court of law. If we tell them what to do differently in the future, who is responsible for their future choices and behavior? We are! If they tell us what they can do differently the next time, who is responsible for their future choices and behavior? They are! Thus it is very important in this process not to answer the question for them. Often, it would be much easier and far more expedient to give them the answer. But when we do that, we take away the chance for them to learn from the experience and to learn to change their choices in the future. We will see the same students back in the office, repeating the same conversation.

Discipline is about teaching children how to behave. We do that by discussing the negative choice, developing alternative choices, and then providing consequences. If we want children to learn self-discipline and to be able to think about their choices, rather than resorting to providing the answer to children, ask some "what" questions. If a student is sent to the office for hitting another student, here's how it might go:

1. What happened?

   I'm in trouble because I hit someone.

2. What caused that to happen?

   I got mad because they took the ball away from me.

3. What could you do differently in the future?

   I don't know.

It is very important that we don't answer the final question for them. Instead, we need to respond with something like this: "I understand how that could have made you angry; however, it is against the school rules to hit someone. So it is very important for you to have a plan of what you will choose to do next time you become angry with someone. In the future, what might happen if you had asked for the ball back? What might happen if you walked away? What might happen if you asked an adult for help?"

After asking three or four "What might happen if…" questions, students should be able to choose one of the suggestions. Once they choose one, talk about how they will go about doing that. After this process, reveal and provide appropriate consequences in a respectful way and then encourage the student to use the new plan in the future.

While it may seem overly simple, this is a very effective process that teaches children to learn from their experiences and mistakes and to make different choices in the future for a more positive outcome.

Home to School Connection

This clear and concise system for a positive school climate is shared with parents at the Fall NEU Parent Forum and the Fall Back-to-School Nights. The system models for parents how routines and structures can be established and how effective this is for student success. We encourage parents to create a similar system at home to support their children's success.

Theory to Practice

✓ Discuss your school climate. What do you think would improve the climate?

✓ Evaluate your school discipline. How much academic time is being lost for discipline incidents? What could you do differently?

✓ What kind of visual reminders could you put in place around the campus?

12

Full Circle

"We never know the love of our parents for us till we have become parents."

~ Henry Ward Beecher

Parenting is one of the most challenging jobs in the world. It is also one of the most important and critical. It comes with the least amount of training and support. Being an effective and involved parent is not something we are born with; it is something we learn through life experiences. When people are born into families with limited parenting skills, without some intervention or training, they will very likely be the same kind of parent that they were raised by. I cannot imagine what my life would have been like if my destiny had not crossed paths with Grandma Meyer. As an adult, when I look back at my early beginnings, I know that my parents loved me very much and were doing the very best that they knew how to do. Often I think they loved me so much they allowed me to be raised by their neighbor around the corner. I am grateful how my life's path worked out. In part because of the adversity and in part because of the incredible love and support of Grandma Meyer and many wonderful teachers, I have been able to become the mother that I always wanted to have to our two daughters. I was very fortunate to meet and marry an amazing life partner, my husband Mike. From the beginning, being effective, involved parents was a priority for us. With the support of friends, and some great schools and staff, we have been able to raise two incredible young women, Lauren, twenty-six, and Marusha, twenty-five, who are both realizing great life success. I'd like you to hear from their perspective about their personal experience with importance of involved parents.

Lauren's Memories

I will never forget the feeling of looking up at the bleachers from my sporting events and seeing my parents there rooting me on. From a very early age, I remember them being involved and supportive in everything I did. When coming home from school, I would get a series of questions. While sometimes I may have given my parents a hard time, it felt truly special to have someone who cared so much about my day. We would go on to discuss what I learned that day and how much schoolwork I had for the night. My parents were never afraid to tell me they expected me to keep up my grades in order to stay involved in my extracurricular activities. We talked about what I wanted to be when I grew up, and college was discussed very early on. My parents also stayed involved in who my current friends were and what we were doing in our spare time.

The way they would communicate never felt they were being nosy in my life. They never told me what friends I could and could not have, but they did establish boundaries and I may remember a little guidance with some of my friend choices. Yet the approach they took made it feel that I was making my own decisions because I didn't want to let them down and I knew they expected more from me. Now as an adult, I look back proudly that I graduated from high school with honors, made it through college in four years, and now have a successful career. I look forward to being an involved parent with my kids when the time comes and will remember the importance of how it felt to have loving, supportive, and involved parents.

Marusha's Memories

I still hold a few memories of my mom screaming and crying. She was screaming and crying because she had two toddlers — eighteen months apart — with no support system to lean on and no resources to refer to. But what I remember more vividly is the turning point in my childhood where my mom stopped screaming. Instead she would talk to me, play with me, laugh with me. What I didn't know at the time is that this was the same moment when my mom took her first parenting class.

Where the "old" mom would have described me as difficult and stubborn, the "new" mom celebrated my high energy and determination and helped me put my unique attributes toward positive experiences and relationships. When I would come home crying from elementary school because I thought my friends were excluding me, the "old" mom would probably think I was being dramatic and brush it off, whereas the "new" mom sat and listened to my feelings and then helped me come up with a plan to resolve the issue the next day at school.

I don't know what I would have done without the guidance of my "new" mom. Through the growing pains of adolescence to making the big decision to transfer colleges and move away from home, my parents were there for me every step of the way, cheering me on, telling me they cared, and giving me guidance when I needed it most.

Have I ever told you, Mom? THANK YOU for taking that parenting class!

Your high energy and determined younger daughter.

Just as the cycle of poverty can be broken with education, so can the cycle of poor parenting. Using differentiated parent support, we need to work effectively with parents to help them to be the best parents they can be so that their children, and our students, can also live their destiny.

APPENDIX

NO EXCUSES
UNIVERSITY

HANDBOOKS

Once you have established a code of conduct based on a common language of character traits, capture the information in handbooks. Create handbooks for staff, students, and parents. These handbooks provide guidelines and specific information to reinforce clarity in climate based on your common language.

STUDENT HANDBOOK
Letter from the Principal

NEU Campus Info:

- ◆ Code of Conduct Expectations
- ◆ Character Violations
- ◆ Classroom Management Plan
- ◆ Character Counts — Six Pillars

College Readiness

- ◆ NEU University Academic
- ◆ MAPS Log
- ◆ Student Goal Organizer
- ◆ Student College Readiness Survey
- ◆ Leadership Opportunities

STAFF NEU ENDORSEMENT
Mission, Vision, Commitment — Who Participates

NEU Campus Info:

- ◆ Code of Conduct
- ◆ Character Counts – Six Pillars
- ◆ Calendar
- ◆ LP Collaboration Commitment

College Readiness

- ◆ NEU University Academic
- ◆ MAPS Log
- ◆ Student Goal Organizer
- ◆ Student College Readiness Survey
- ◆ Leadership Opportunities

continued

PARENT HANDBOOK

Letter from the Principal
Mission, Vision, Commitment
Who Participates

NEU Campus Info:

- ◆ Code of Conduct
- ◆ Daily Schedule
- ◆ Events Calendar
- ◆ To & From School
- ◆ Meeting Student Needs
- ◆ Health Info

Parent Information:

- ◆ Parent Code of Conduct
- ◆ Parent Education
- ◆ Parent Endorsement
- ◆ Volunteer
- ◆ Resources

College Readiness

- ◆ TAKE 5
- ◆ A-G College Requirement
- ◆ Accountability
- ◆ Student Goal
- ◆ Parent Goal
- ◆ College Financing
- ◆ Student Leadership Opportunities

Dear Students,

Welcome to the No Excuses University at Los Peñasquitos. "No Excuses is not just our motto; it is our commitment as students, parents, and staff to do whatever it takes for you to be successful in school. This year you will learn like never before as you prepare your path to college. Each and every one of you has very special academic and social gifts which you use daily as you work hard in all subject areas. They are also seen in the way that you display character by focusing on the six character traits described in this handbook. As you read through this handbook, you will learn about the expectations we have for all students of the No Excuses University at Los Pen. I know that you are capable of being a great student and promise that you will be successful if you remember these two words, No Excuses. I am proud of you and look forward to supporting your learning and celebrating your successes throughout the 2010-2011 school year.

Sincerely,
Mrs. McLaughlin
Principal

No Excuses University
at Los Peñasquitos
Student Handbook

This book belongs to:

_____

The year I graduate college:

_____

No Excuses University
Code of Conduct

At Los Pen, we take student safety and good student behavior very seriously. We only have a few rules, but these rules apply any time students are on campus, traveling to and from school, or on a school-sponsored field trip or activity. School staff members, students, and parents all share responsibility for good student behavior. The school has the responsibility to clearly communicate and enforce student behavior in a fair, consistent, and supportive manner. Parents have the responsibility to reinforce the expectations of the school and to help their children become responsible citizens. Students have the responsibility to follow the code of conduct and to make good choices.

Our Code of Conduct

All students will be asked to follow the Los Pen Code of Conduct. The students will be asked to sign a poster hanging in the class committing to the Los Pen Code of Conduct.

I WILL BE TRUSTWORTHY
I WILL BE RESPECTFUL
I WILL BE RESPONSIBLE
I WILL BE FAIR
I WILL BE CARING
I WILL BE A GOOD CITIZEN

Character Counts! Awards

Character Counts! Awards will be given to students when they demonstrate good conduct and responsible behavior. All adults on staff may give them out as appropriate. Character Counts! Awards will be randomly selected from each classroom to be announced at Friday Flag.

CHARACTER VIOLATIONS

CHARACTER VIOLATIONS

Character Violations are used to record disciplinary instances when students violate The Los Pen Code of Conduct. A copy of the Character Violation will be sent home for the parent to sign and return to school the following day.

<u>*First Character Violation*</u> – Student sent to the office, call home, discussion with teacher, and possible loss of recess or other appropriate consequence.

<u>*Second Character Violation*</u> – Student sent to the office, call home, teacher conference to discuss behavior interventions, disciplinary action.

<u>*Third Character Violation*</u> – Student sent to the office, disciplinary action, individual student behavior contract, parent teacher conference.

CONSEQUENCES

Any Los Peñasquitos staff member may choose to issue a natural or logical consequence in any situation where it would be appropriate. Character Violations will be referred to the office for further disciplinary actions. If parents or guardians have any questions they may contact the office.

continued

THINGS TO KEEP AT HOME

1. Do not bring gum to school.

2. Personal items. These include, but are not limited to:

    ◆ Any toys, including items such as trading cards

    ◆ Electronic devices, such as Ipods, MP3 players, and handheld video games

    ◆ Sports equipment, such as footballs, basketballs, tennis balls, or soccer balls

    ◆ Anything with wheels (skates, skateboards, scooters, and heely shoes)

3. Weapons, or simulated weapons, may NEVER be brought to school. These include, but are not limited to, squirt guns, air powered guns, knives, pocket knives, explosives, and all other dangerous objects.

PHONES

Phones must be off during the school day, including during BLAST and/or ESS.

FOOD

Due to many food allergies, you may not share food or snacks. Food may only be shared when supervised by a staff member for class parties and/or birthdays.

CROSSWALK AND PARKING LOT

Students walking to and from school must use the school crosswalk and stay on the sidewalks surrounding the parking lot.

CHARACTER COUNTS
SIX PILLARS

TRUSTWORTHINESS

- ◆ Be honest
- ◆ Don't deceive, cheat or steal
- ◆ Be reliable — do what you say you'll do
- ◆ Have the courage to do the right thing
- ◆ Build a good reputation
- ◆ Be loyal — stand by your family, friends, and country

RESPECT

- ◆ Treat others with respect; follow the Golden Rule
- ◆ Be tolerant of differences
- ◆ Use good manners, not bad language
- ◆ Be considerate of the feelings of others
- ◆ Don't threaten, hit, or hurt anyone
- ◆ Deal peacefully with anger, insults, and disagreements

RESPONSIBILITY

- ◆ Do what you are supposed to do
- ◆ Persevere: keep on trying!
- ◆ Always do your best
- ◆ Use self-control
- ◆ Be self-disciplined
- ◆ Think before you act — consider the consequences
- ◆ Be accountable for your choices

continued

Character Counts
Six Pillars *(continued)*

Fairness

- Play by the rules
- Take turns and share
- Be open-minded; listen to others
- Don't take advantage of others
- Don't blame others carelessly

Caring

- Be kind
- Be compassionate and show you care
- Express gratitude
- Forgive others
- Help people in need

Citizenship

- Do your share to make your school and community better
- Cooperate
- Get involved in community affairs
- Stay informed; vote
- Be a good neighbor
- Obey laws and rules
- Respect authority
- Protect the environment

NO EXCUSES

CLASSROOM MANAGEMENT PLAN
(GRADES 2-5)

*"Character is doing the right thing,
even when no one is watching"*

CODE OF CONDUCT:

I will be trustworthy.   I will be respectful.   I will be fair.
I will be responsible.   I will be a good citizen.   I will be caring.

If you choose to break the code of conduct (consequences):

1ST TIME: **CAUTION: YELLOW**
Sign in the book.

2ND TIME: **STOP: RED**
Sign in the book. Fill out the rethinking paper

3RD TIME: **TIME-OUT:**
Sign in the Book
Take a Break in another class
Fill out the time-out letter/home to parent
Possible Loss of Recess

4TH TIME OR SEVERE DISRUPTION:
Immediately sent to the office
Fill out character violation

POSITIVE REINFORCEMENT:
Praise — Daily
Positive Notes Home — Random
Character Counts Award
Individual Classroom Reinforcement

We have read and discussed this classroom management plan and
will support and honor the plan throughout the year.

_____   _____

Parent Signature   Student Signature

RETHINKING LETTER

You are receiving a second warning about your negative choices. Please think about what you have done and answer these questions.

1. What did I do to receive my yellow warning?

   _____

   _____

2. What did I do to receive my red warning?

   _____

   _____

3. How did your choice affect others?

   _____

   _____

4. What caused your negative choice?

   _____

   _____

5. What could you do better next time?

   _____

   _____

Please check one:

_____ I get the point. I will try harder in class.

_____ I don't understand. We need to talk about my
          behavior.

_____   _____
Parent Signature   Student Signature

NO EXCUSES UNIVERSITY
ACADEMIC EXPECTATIONS

At the No Excuses University at Los Pen we have high expectations for all students and believe if students work hard they will be successful. In addition, we would like to provide all students at Los Pen with the academic and social skills necessary to be successful in middle school and high school, and be prepared to go to college.

ACADEMIC HONESTY

In support of the District's Academic Honesty Policy, students are expected to demonstrate acts of honesty at all times. Teachers and staff members will support and enforce all district rules of academic honesty and provide a learning environment that does not tolerate dishonesty. Any student who violates the rules of the Academic Honesty Policy will be subject to disciplinary action.

ATTENDANCE

It is important to be on time and attend school every day. If you are not able to attend school you should remind your parents to call the office. In addition, you should also speak to your teacher to find out what work you missed when you were gone. When you miss school you miss out!

TAKE FIVE

Expect your family to take 5 minutes
EVERY DAY to discuss your day at school!

1. What is your student goal?
2. What did you do today to help achieve your student goal?
3. How did you make character count today?
4. What can you do tomorrow to conduct yourself as a No Excuses University student?
5. Encourage your child in a very specific and genuine way.

THIRD GRADE
STUDENT GOAL ORGANIZER

Name: _____

Date: _____

Term: _____

MATH: _____

My **MATH** score goal for the trimester is:_____

The things I can do to work on my goal this term are:

    1. _____

    2. _____

    3. _____

READING: _____

My **READING** score goal for the trimester is:_____

The things I can do to work on my goal this term are:

    1. _____

    2. _____

    3. _____

LANGUAGE USAGE: _____

My **LANGUAGE USAGE** score goal for the trimester is:_____

The things I can do to work on my goal this term are:

    1. _____

    2. _____

    3. _____

_____   _____

Student Signature   Teacher Signature

MAP

MAP (Measure of Academic Progress) is a three-part test covering Reading, Language Usage, and Math. Using a computer, all students in grades 2-5 will take the MAP test in the fall, winter, and spring. Your teacher will use MAP scores throughout the year to measure your growth in Reading, Language Usage, and Math.

READING

	160	170	180	190	200	210	220	230	240	250	260
Fall											
Winter											
Spring											

LANGUAGE

	160	170	180	190	200	210	220	230	240	250	260
Fall											
Winter											
Spring											

MATH

	160	170	180	190	200	210	220	230	240	250	260
Fall											
Winter											
Spring											

STUDENT COLLEGE READINESS SURVEY

1. What do I want to learn this year at Los Pen to prepare for college?

   _____

   _____

   _____

   _____

   _____

2. What did I learn this year at Los Pen to prepare for college?

   _____

   _____

   _____

   _____

   _____

3. What year will I graduate from college?

   _____

NEU LEADERSHIP
OPPORTUNITIES

Student Council Officers & Representatives (4-5)

The Student Council members will coordinate student council fundraisers and spirit days.

Character Crew Club (3-5)

The Character Crew Club will focus on the six character traits, promoting safety, conflict resolution, and community service. The club is student led with the help of our Student Services staff. Third, fourth, and fifth grade students will learn positive ways to promote character, handle conflict resolution, and perform community service throughout the year. The students will also have the opportunity to work in committees and develop leadership skills.

5th Grade Safety Patrol

Fifth grade students will assist students to get to and from school safely.

No Excuses University Student Leaders (2-5)

NEU Students will have the opportunity to participate in a variety of leadership opportunities throughout the year.

Explicit Examples of Behaviors

Day	Area of Behavior	What it looks like	What it doesn't look like
1	Character Counts!	• All six traits	• Breaking the code of conduct
2	Walking/waiting in line	• Voice level 0 in halls • Walk quietly • Keep hands and feet to yourself • Face forward • Space between you & the person in front of you	• Touching/kicking the walls • Touching/kicking others • Running • Dilly dallying
3	Assemblies	• Come in quietly • Sit where directed by adults • Eyes on speaker • Raise hand to speak • Look to your teachers for dismissal	• Running in • Ignoring adults • Looking around at the room • Calling out • Getting up without teacher's direction
4	After school & dismissal	• Walk in line with classmates • Wait to be dismissed by your teacher • Go to proper designated area • Walk to ESS, BLAST, your parents, or directly home • Focus on task	• Running ahead of class • Leaving without saying goodbye to teacher • Playing on playground or front of the school • Talking with friends • Going home a different way
5	Playground rules	• Review and follow the rules • Solve conflicts respectfully • Good sportsmanship • Get help from adult when needed • Listen to the yard duties	• Ignoring the rules • Cheating, bragging, complaining • Ignoring the yard duties • Physical aggression • Shouting to solve a conflict • Going out of designated areas

#		Expectations	Behaviors
6	**ACADEMIC EXPECTATIONS**	◆ Always do your best ◆ Complete and return homework ◆ Work in class ◆ Cooperate in group work	◆ Not trying ◆ Forgetting homework ◆ Daydreaming, talking, wasting time ◆ Being bossy in groups or not helping
7	**END OF DAY PACKING UP**	◆ Quietly get backpack ◆ Put papers in the backpack ◆ Carry or wear your backpack	◆ Talking or playing while getting backpack ◆ Forgetting papers ◆ Twirling or swinging backpack
8	**CAFETERIA**	◆ Keep your area clean ◆ Come prepared ◆ Keep voices down ◆ Respect yard duties ◆ Follow cafeteria expectations ◆ Use your manners	◆ Throwing food ◆ Loud talking ◆ Running around ◆ Disrespecting yard duties ◆ Wasting food
9	**HALLWAY**	◆ Go directly to your destination ◆ Keep hallways clean ◆ Walk quietly ◆ Keep hands and feet to yourself	◆ Touching/kicking the walls ◆ Touching/kicking others ◆ Running ◆ Dilly dallying
10	**TRANSITIONS TO AND FROM CLASSROOMS**	◆ Take materials you need ◆ Wait in line quietly until teacher invites you into their room ◆ Respect other student's things	◆ Playing in line ◆ Talking loudly and bothering other classes ◆ Playing in someone's desk
11	**BATHROOM ETIQUETTE/ PROCEDURES**	◆ Always flush ◆ Wait patiently for a stall ◆ Return to class promptly	◆ Wasting water and paper ◆ Looking in the stalls ◆ Playing around

continued

EXPLICIT EXAMPLES OF BEHAVIORS *continued*

DAY	AREA OF BEHAVIOR	WHAT IT LOOKS LIKE	WHAT IT DOESN'T LOOK LIKE
12	GUESTS & PHONE PROCEDURES	◆ Keep working ◆ If there is not work available take out a book and read quietly	◆ Watching guest ◆ Listening to adult conversation ◆ Talking to friends or playing
13	INTERACTING WITH PEERS	◆ All six traits ◆ Resolving conflict with respect ◆ Being loyal ◆ Being helpful ◆ Forgiveness	◆ Breaking the code of conduct ◆ Gossiping ◆ Holding grudges ◆ Getting others to dislike another person
14	TALKING WITH AND GREETING ADULTS	◆ Stop and face the person ◆ Eye contact ◆ Listen ◆ Respond respectfully	◆ Keep walking ◆ Looking around ◆ Ignoring ◆ Arguing
15	VOICE LEVEL – (1 TO 10)	◆ Use appropriate voice levels in different areas of campus and during class ◆ Speak respectfully to others ◆ Silent (0) means NO talking at all	◆ Yelling or talking to loudly in the halls, bathroom, or in class ◆ Sassy or rude comments ◆ Whispering when told to be silent
16	BEHAVIOR IN OFFICE	◆ Walk in quietly ◆ Wait for conversation to stop before speaking ◆ Speak quietly ◆ Use manners	◆ Run in to the office ◆ Interrupt conversation ◆ Talk so loudly they can't hold phone conversations ◆ Demand attention

17	CLASSROOM MATERIALS	◆ Use supplies sparingly ◆ Put supplies away ◆ Handle gently ◆ Turn pages carefully	◆ Wasteful use ◆ Leave supplies out ◆ Throwing supplies ◆ Rough handling
18	REVIEW CLASSROOM MANAGEMENT		
19	GUEST TEACHER BEHAVIOR	◆ Follow same class rules ◆ Exceptional manners ◆ One student provides help at a time ◆ Take initiative in helping out ◆ Keep each other accountable ◆ Stay on task	◆ Changing the rules ◆ Talking and fooling around ◆ Blurting out answers ◆ Several students tell the teacher what to do ◆ Purposely creating problems ◆ Off task
20	RAINY DAY BEHAVIOR	◆ Stay dry ◆ Be careful with umbrellas ◆ Walk into MPR ◆ Sit at table until excused ◆ Voice level 2 or 3 in MPR ◆ Follow lunch expectations	◆ Play in puddles ◆ Twirling and playing with umbrellas ◆ Running around ◆ Disrespecting yard duties ◆ Yelling and fooling around

The fiftieth school to join the NEU Network of Schools, Kyrene de los Niños is an elementary school in Tempe, Arizona that adopted the Los Peñ's School Climate System and then took it a step further. The staff not only created a climate that capitalized on a proactive approach to teaching behavior, but also developed a comprehensive form with descriptions of what each behavior looks like and doesn't look like. Such a step supports consistency that is appreciated by parents and deserved by students. A copy of this chart can also be found on the CD.

185

PARENT INVOLVEMENT SYSTEM

- Form a committee. Include administration, staff, and parents Parent Liaisons (district)
- Paid Full-time Parent Liaisons on Title I (Campus)
- Needs Assessment
- Parent Survey
- Staff Training
- Community Resources Training
- Parent Ambassadors
- Award "Very Involved Parents" with V.I.P. Award
- Home visits

Communication

- School info packets given by hospital at birth
- Website for district and school with current events
- Automated phone system
- Text messages
- Newsletters and e-mail
- Parent electronic access to grades, homework, and attendance
- Public Service Announcement with a child's voice
- Monthly meetings
- Parent Ambassadors
- Invite parent volunteers to help with phone calls to families

Parent and Family Activities

Frequent opportunities for parents to come to school

- Multi-cultural events
- Movie Night
- Writing Camps
- Field trips to universities
- Open House
- Summer Family Enrichment Program
- PTA's, PTO's, Booster Clubs
- Ice Cream Socials
- Bingo for Books (district)
- Open door policy for lunch
- Watch Dogs – Father Volunteers (campus)
- Smiling dads – program where dads open the doors in morning and greet students

continued

Parent Involvement System *(continued)*

Parent University

Provide food and childcare

- Recognition or credit for parents going to activities
- Hold events where they live
- Parent training on movie media and shared by DVD or the Internet
- Parent Café
- Guided Reading Workshop to teach parents how to help their child learn to read
- Family Literacy Festival
- Parenting Training - Speakers (that address parents needs)
- "Math - Make & Take"
- Love & Logic
- Parental involvement conference for parents with breakout sessions (district)
- The Importance of Fathers
- 40 Developmental Assets
- Building Confident Families
- Gang Awareness, Drug Awareness, Weapon Safety, Internet Safety

Community Education Classes for Parents

- Adult education options on campus on evenings or Saturdays, ESL, computer skills, GED, career planning, financial planning
- Citizenship classes
- Spanish Literacy
- Technology trainings in partnership with Attorney Generals office
- Financial Aid – partner with Chamber of Commerce or other community agency
- Arts and crafts
- Nutrition classes
- Parent cooking class
- Preschooler Day – day with librarian & mother reading books (campus)

Family Support

- Parent Resource Center
- Health and Resource Fairs with parents, businesses, community
- Sister Schools (district) partner affluent with low-income schools
- Clothes Closet (district)
- Holiday Assistance
- Food Bank or Closet
- Backpack Programs

BIBLIOGRAPHY

Committee for Children. 2011. "Committee for Children." Accessed February 20, 2011. www.cfchildren.org

Empowering People, Inc. 2011. "Developing Capable Young People." Accessed, February 20, 2011. www.capabilitiesinc.com.

Josephson Institute. 2011. "Character education program: Character Counts." Accessed February 20, 2011. www.charactercounts.org

King, Jeff, and Damen Lopez. 2008. *TurnAround Schools: Creating Cultures of Universal Achievement.* Turnaround Schools Publishing.

Lopez, Damen. 2009. *No Excuses University*. Ramona, CA: TurnAround Schools Publications.

Maslow, Abraham. 1954. *Motivation and Personality*. New York: Harper and Bros.

ABOUT TURNAROUND SCHOOLS

Damen Lopez founded TurnAround Schools in 2006. Damen and Dan Lopez base their work upon the following two principles:

1. Every child has the right to be prepared to attend college.
2. It is the responsibility of adults in the school to develop exceptional systems that make that dream a reality.

TurnAround Schools organizes Institutes where practitioners from remarkable schools share how they coax impressive success from traditionally at-risk learners. Teachers and leaders leave our Institutes with solid strategies they can put into place the next day, and a hopeful optimism for the potential of each of their students.

Additionally, Damen Lopez and TurnAround Schools Associates provide direct, personalized, on-site assistance and training for schools and districts.

Our mission is to empower educators with proven strategies that get results. We can help your teachers and leaders implement these strategies. We are successful at what we do.

For more information, please visit www.TurnAroundSchools.com or email us at info@TurnAroundSchools.com

ACKNOWLEDGEMENTS

The book that you are holding in your hands would never have happened without the helping hands of many others I am grateful to acknowledge.

When our paths crossed in 2002, I had absolutely no idea of the journey I would travel on with Damen Lopez. His amazing passion, creativity, and dedication to quality education with the belief in a universal achievement for all students, has inspired me to become a better person, educator, and professional. And also an author! Several years ago putting my ideas on paper was a challenge from Damen. Without his encouragement, support, writing expertise and the occasional "kick in the behind," this book would never have become a reality. During our journey he has become one of my dearest, lifetime friends.

I am grateful to the Los Pen staff that has worked so diligently to create a "No Excuses" culture and a belief that all students can be successful. Your commitment to students is the model for all of the No Excuses University network schools; it all started with you. The staff's collaboration and expertise are a very large part of the strategies and practices shared in this book. Thank you for your professionalism and friendship.

I have been inspired by many of our No Excuses University network schools. Particularly, San Jacinto, Dove Elementary, Kyrene de Los Niños and La Granada, who enhanced some concepts and ideas from

TurnAround Schools and made them even better. Additionally, they have created many new ideas that they have generously shared and some of which are included in this book.

I have several supporting editors/friends/cheerleaders to thank. In particular there are three ladies who have supported me every step of the way. They have listened to me worry and whine and helped relieve my stress during this process by always being there to listen and to help find moments to laugh. They encouraged me and took the time to read every word, providing helpful feedback and guidance. Deanne McLaughlin, Kim Melvin, and Kelley Magill – thank you for being part of my life and particularly for helping me make it to the finish line with this book.

I would have never had the opportunity to work with parents so closely without the mentorship, encouragement and support from three dedicated educators, Suzanne Roy, Elaine Cofrancesco, and Peggy Hetherington. They all saw the potential in me to become a counselor and their guidance and belief in me helped make that a reality.

I am indebted to the professionals who took my work and used their expertise to make it printworthy. Kaitlin Barr for editing (kaitlin.n.barr@gmail.com); Shendl Diamond for her layout design (LikeMindsPress.com); Catherine Perry for her cover design (CPerryDesigns.com), and Dan Lopez, President of TurnAround Schools. Dan, along with his brother Damen, believed in my work enough to insist that it needed to be put on paper and published to share with others. Thank you for your tremendous patience and support throughout this endeavor.

I want to acknowledge my parents for loving me enough to let me go around the corner to live with Grandma Meyer. I am grateful to Grandma Meyer for opening her home and heart and helping me become the person that I am today. A special thanks to my brother, David, for all of those Sunday evening walks around the corner escorting me to my safe haven of the Meyer home and for continuing to be my loving big brother.

Grandma Meyer used to tell me that patience is a virtue, so I must thank my very virtuous family, including "my two boys," who had a lot of opportunities to practice patience while I struggled with writing this book. Along with their patience they provided their love. More importantly they helped me learn how to be a better person and a parent.

ABOUT THE AUTHOR

Fran Hjalmarson has more than twenty years' experience as an educator. Using innovative and comprehensive approaches as a school counselor, Fran has achieved highly successful results at several elementary schools. Known to her students and families simply as "Mrs. H," Fran is committed to supporting the social/emotional needs of her students in a way that facilitates academic success at the same time. Utilizing innovative and effective strategies, Fran has been able to positively impact the parent involvement and community outreach at Los Peñasquitos Elementary School. Highly skilled at providing interventions that align with a detailed Response to Intervention model, Fran works with educators across the country in an effort to support success for all students and families.

Fran currently works for Poway Unified School District as school counselor at Los Peñasquitos Elementary in San Diego, California. During the summer and throughout the year, Fran works for TurnAround Schools as an educational consultant.

Living in Poway, California, she has been married to her husband, Mike, for 28 years. They have raised two amazing daughters, Lauren and Marusha, who live within miles of them in the San Diego area with their partners.